The Price of Forgetting

The Price of Forgetting

How Subscriptions Steal Our Money and Minds

(Reclaiming Financial Clarity in a World of Automatic Spending)

Evelyn Hawthorne

Mindful Pages

Published in 2025

ISBN: 9789371771511 (PB)
ISBN: 9789371776691 (eBook)

Published by

Mindful Pages
Imprint of Alpha Editions LLC
312 W. 2nd St #1834
Casper, WY 82601, USA

Content

The introduction
The Age of Forgetting

The modern marketplace hums with an almost imperceptible rhythm, a steady exchange that takes place beyond the reach of our conscious notice. Day after day, money slips from our accounts—not with a deliberate signature, not even with a moment's pause for thought, but through the quiet machinery of recurring payments. Subscriptions, memberships, trial offers that slide seamlessly into charges, and digital services that tug at our wallets with each cycle. This is not the dramatic outflow of sudden expenditure but something more insidious: a slow, constant siphoning that reshapes not just our balance sheets but the very ways we think, feel, and behave.

This book begins with a disquieting observation. The money we lose through subscription models is not simply gone in the financial sense; its disappearance signals a deeper phenomenon—psychological, emotional, cultural. It tells us something about how we have come to engage with value, ownership, and selfhood in a world enthralled by the promise of seamless consumption. What follows is not a handbook of penny-pinching tips, nor an austere guide to budgeting. It is, instead, a challenge: to reconsider the foundations of our financial consciousness and to shift from passive drifting to deliberate stewardship—not only of money, but of attention.

Why do we tolerate this quiet erosion of agency? Why do the creeping charges provoke so little alarm? The answer lies less in individual forgetfulness than in the architecture of forgetting deliberately built into subscription economies. These systems are engineered to bypass scrutiny, to turn expenditure into background noise, and to foster a psychological state where financial commitment is automated, unquestioned, and—most dangerously—invisible. What takes hold is not mere absentmindedness but a cultivated numbness, a "monetary anaesthesia" that blunts our sensitivity to what is lost each month, and to what choices have been silently foreclosed.

Forgetting, here, is not accident but strategy. It mirrors a broader cultural shift: from ownership to access, permanence to perpetual rental. Once, to possess was to anchor oneself in stability, to locate value in the tangible, the lasting. Now, possession is displaced by endless streams of licences, by fleeting permissions to use, to watch, to borrow. The shift has consequences beyond the material. It destabilises our relationship with possessions, untethers our sense of security, and corrodes the clarity that comes from knowing precisely what is ours and what it costs us to hold it. In the subscription age, value itself dissolves into something transient, something curiously hollow.

But the consequences of this trend reach beyond bank accounts. Subscriptions are not just conduits for money—they colonise habits, capture attention, and weave themselves into the fibres of identity. They thrive on our vulnerabilities: the tendency to forget, the seduction of micro-commitments that seem harmless in isolation, the yearning for a personalised sense of belonging. Algorithms feed us illusions of necessity and exclusivity, re-casting us not simply as consumers but as characters in a story about who we are, or who we might wish to become.

The emotional undercurrents of this phenomenon are equally profound. Many subscriptions function as palliatives for loneliness, for boredom, for the aching void of uncertainty. They masquerade as sources of comfort, delivering fleeting bursts of gratification while disguising the compulsions that drive them. The abundance of choice, especially in the digital sphere, paradoxically fuels a sense of fatigue. Freedom itself becomes oppressive, leaving us disenchanted, oddly unsatisfied. In this climate, spending is rarely about genuine selection; it becomes a kind of reflexive attempt to soothe—an attempt destined, inevitably, to fail.

What this book proposes is a reframing of budgeting: not as a sterile exercise in arithmetic, nor as a punitive regime of restraint, but as a form of narrative therapy. Budgeting, here, becomes an ethical practice, a way to push back against the tide of passive consumption and to reclaim agency through memory, reflection, and clarity. It asks us to listen to the stories we tell ourselves through our financial habits, to examine the silent messages inscribed in every line of a bank statement, every recurring debit, every impulse purchase.

Such reflection reveals more than figures; it exposes shame, silence, and the tangled emotions that so often shroud financial choices. By breaking these patterns—by naming them with compassion rather than judgment—we open space for freedom, for alignment between what we spend and what we value most deeply.

On a larger scale, the subscription economy is not merely clever business strategy; it represents a subtle form of servitude. Consumers are rendered into products, their behaviours mined for data and monetised by corporations whose interests are rarely congruent with personal autonomy. The model extends beyond media and entertainment, seeping into housing, education, even knowledge itself. To recognise this encroachment is to see the urgency of reclaiming ethical agency—not just for the sake of private accounts, but for the shape of the societies we inhabit.

The traps themselves are worth examining in detail: the seductive hooks of trial offers, the seamless retention designs, the gamified loyalty schemes that keep us tethered. To unmask these strategies is to regain some measure of defence. But practical tactics alone are insufficient. Each pound spent is a tacit vote for a system, for a value, for a future. Budgeting thus emerges as more than personal discipline—it becomes activism, an assertion of conscience that aligns money with meaning, private choices with public consequences.

The vision offered here is not dour. It gestures towards a form of budgeting alive to context, to mood, to the ebb and flow of life itself. It suggests pruning subscriptions not merely to save money, but to preserve vitality. It encourages cultivating joy and presence in spending decisions, modelling for future generations a way to navigate the digital reflex with awareness and creativity rather than resignation.

At its heart, *The Price of Forgetting* is an act of remembrance. To remember what we spend and why. To recall who we are beneath the sediment of automated charges and algorithmic nudges. To see clarity itself as currency, memory as a financial asset, attention as wealth. The challenge is to pierce the spell of invisibility, to transform budgeting from a chore into a practice of sovereignty—over money, yes, but also over the self.

What follows, then, is an exploration of the true costs of subscription culture—measured not only in pounds but in attention, in freedom, in identity itself. It is a call to resist the quiet erosion of agency, to awaken from the lull of automation, and to chart a path towards financial clarity and emotional resilience in a world all too ready to make us forget.

Chapter 1
The Drift Toward Automatic Living

The drift from deliberate budgeting towards automatic spending is one of the quiet revolutions of modern financial life—profound, yet oddly underexamined. Where once we balanced income against outgoings with care, weighing priorities and wrestling with choices, today much of this labour has been surrendered. Algorithms and autopay systems take the reins, accompanied by the soothing reassurance of "set it and forget it." What masquerades as convenience conceals something more troubling: a surrender of intentionality, often unconscious, to infrastructures not designed merely to serve but to capture, monetise, and, in subtle ways, domesticate our financial attention.

Here lies a paradox worth dwelling on. Automation promises freedom, a release from the tedium of paying bills and tracking due dates. Yet with that freedom comes distance: an estrangement from the very decisions that give shape to our economic lives. When money drifts silently from our accounts—subscriptions inked into existence long ago, forgotten but endlessly renewed—spending itself loses its edge of recognition. This softening effect, what might aptly be called *monetary anaesthesia*, dulls our sensitivity to costs. It silences the small jolt that once attended an act of payment, the necessary discomfort that sharpens financial awareness. Automation makes everything seamless, but in that ease lies a psychological price: indifference. How often do we hear stories of people realising, with shock, that hundreds or even thousands have bled away into services no longer useful, no longer even remembered? These are not aberrations; they are the inevitable result of invisibility, an invisibility carefully cultivated to benefit companies far more than customers.

But the matter is not only one of perception. Beneath it runs a deeper cultural current: the shift from ownership to access. Buying outright carried with it a sense of permanence, a tether of responsibility and, often, affection. Owning meant control, however modest. Subscription, by contrast, grants only provisional rights: the right to use, to view, to listen—for as long as the payments flow. This shift reconfigures our relationship to value itself. Permanence is replaced by impermanence, and with it vanish the anchors that once supported thoughtful engagement with what we consumed. Philosophers and economists alike have remarked on this erosion of attachment. When nothing is truly ours, our patterns of consumption become lighter, more disposable, less considered. Convenience flourishes, yes, but at the cost of depth.

And it is convenience that sits at the heart of the matter. It is no accident that sign-ups are frictionless, renewals nearly invisible, cancellations buried in labyrinthine menus. The very smoothness of the experience is weaponised, turning our desire for ease into a vulnerability. When the act of spending is reduced to a few taps—or, more insidiously, to no act at all—it bypasses the neural circuits of reflection. What should be a moment of choice becomes a default. To name it bluntly: convenience, so prized in modern life, is not neutral. It is a design, a manoeuvre. And the toll it exacts is autonomy itself.

This chapter follows these threads deliberately, though not always neatly. We will unravel the myth of control promised by automated budgeting, probe the cognitive consequences of invisible spending, interrogate the philosophical loss embedded in the decline of ownership, and question the trade-offs convenience demands. The aim is not only analysis but preparation: to furnish readers with a language and framework for recognising the forces shaping their financial habits, and, more importantly, to reclaim agency where it has quietly slipped away.

As you move forward, pause for a moment over your own recurring payments. Consider how many tick away, unseen, beneath the surface of your financial life. Ask whether the ease of automation has insulated you not only from inconvenience but also from intention. For what is at stake here is larger than mere money. The drift toward automatic living is no trivial technical innovation; it is a cultural, psychological shift with far-reaching implications. To see it clearly is already to resist it. And resistance, in this case, takes a simple but radical form: transforming budgeting from background noise into a conscious act of self-governance.

This chapter is, in essence, an invitation to confront those hidden currents—currents that would prefer you forget—and to begin the slow, deliberate work of remembering.

The Myth of Control

The idea that we control our money is one of the most persistent illusions of modern financial life. Few phrases capture this myth more succinctly than the mantra "set it and forget it," a seductive promise embedded in every automatic payment, subscription service, and autopay system we use. It suggests that budgeting has evolved into a seamless, effortless routine—one where our financial obligations manage themselves, freeing us from the cognitive burden of constant vigilance. Yet beneath this veneer of convenience lies a profound psychological vulnerability: in relinquishing active engagement, we surrender not just control over our money, but the very awareness that underpins prudent financial decision-making.

The digital economy, with its endless array of subscription-based services and automated payment platforms, has fundamentally transformed budgeting from a deliberate, reflective practice into a largely passive, almost invisible process. This shift is far from trivial. Traditionally, managing one's finances required conscious attention—calculating expenses, prioritising spending, and adjusting habits based on fluctuating circumstances. Today, much of that work has been ceded to technology designed to operate quietly in the background. While this promises to reduce cognitive load and prevent late fees, it also erodes the mental models necessary for understanding where money goes and why.

This erosion begins with the *illusion of control* itself. People frequently overestimate their ability to monitor automated payments because these systems feel reliable and "set-and-forget" sounds like mastery over one's finances. However, studies in behavioural economics and psychology have demonstrated that when tasks become automated, individuals are prone to cognitive disengagement. In financial contexts, this means the brain stops actively encoding the experience of spending. Without the conscious act of authorising each transaction, the expenditure loses its emotional and cognitive salience. This phenomenon resembles what some scholars call "payment decoupling," where spending is detached from the physical or mental cues—such as handing over cash or typing in card details—that normally trigger spending awareness.

The consequences are striking. Consider the case of Jane, a working professional who, like millions, signed up for various streaming, fitness, and learning subscriptions during moments of enthusiasm or social influence. Over the years, many of these services fell out of use, but the recurring charges persisted. Because these payments were automated, Jane rarely noticed their ongoing deduction from her account until an unexpected overdraft alerted her. She was not alone; a growing body of anecdotal and empirical evidence reveals that forgotten subscriptions quietly drain hundreds, sometimes thousands, of pounds annually from consumers' finances. This invisibility of spending does not merely risk financial loss—it fosters a kind of *monetary anaesthesia*, dulling sensitivity to the ongoing outflows and eroding the feedback loops critical to budgeting.

Moreover, the myth of control obscures the strategic design choices of companies operating in the digital economy. Businesses understand that once a customer enrols in an automatic payment system, inertia and the effort required to cancel create a behavioural lock-in. The simplicity of signing up contrasts sharply with the complexity of opting out, a discrepancy that exploits human tendencies toward procrastination and avoidance. This dynamic reveals that "set it and forget it" functions less as a consumer empowerment tool and more as a psychological trap. It displaces responsibility from active choice to passive acquiescence, turning budgeting into a default behaviour governed by corporate convenience rather than individual intention.

Beyond the psychological dimension, this shift invites a broader reflection on what budgeting means in an economy built on subscription models. Historically, budgeting implied a relationship of stewardship—allocating finite resources according to needs, desires, and values, each expenditure a conscious affirmation or denial. Automation disrupts this stewardship by outsourcing financial decision-making to software algorithms and corporate billing cycles. This transfer has philosophical implications. It suggests a relinquishment of agency, a surrendering of ownership over one's economic narrative. What is lost in this drift is not only money but the cognitive architecture of financial self-awareness, the capacity to deliberate, adjust, and grow through engagement with one's financial flows.

Critics of automated billing might argue that convenience is a necessary trade-off in a complex modern world. Indeed, the benefits are undeniable: reduced mental load, avoidance of late payments, and streamlined cash flow management. Yet accepting convenience uncritically risks ignoring its hidden costs. The psychological complacency induced by automation creates fertile ground for overconsumption, as invisible charges accumulate unchecked. More insidiously, it fosters a disengagement from one's financial reality that diminishes resilience and adaptive capacity. When the unexpected occurs—a job loss, a change in priorities, or a sudden expense—those who have ceded control to automation may find themselves ill-equipped to respond effectively.

This vulnerability is compounded by the sheer proliferation of subscription services. The digital economy encourages microtransactions and low-friction enrolments, each designed to seem insignificant alone but cumulative in effect. The mental overhead required to track and evaluate dozens of monthly payments quickly becomes prohibitive, further incentivising passive automation. In this environment, the notion of control becomes a mirage, a comforting fiction that allows consumers to defer engagement indefinitely while their financial health quietly deteriorates.

Reclaiming control demands a reorientation of budgeting from passive automation back to active engagement. This does not necessitate abandoning technology or convenience wholesale, but rather integrating tools and habits that restore visibility and intentionality. For example, regular financial audits focused on recurring payments, setting explicit limits on subscription spending, or employing apps that flag dormant or underused services can counteract the drift toward invisibility. Crucially, fostering a mindset that views budgeting as an ongoing dialogue with one's values and goals, rather than a one-off task, reestablishes the cognitive feedback loops automation tends to disrupt.

Ultimately, the myth of control is a cautionary tale about the limits of convenience and the dangers of disengagement. It challenges us to reconsider the promises of automation and to confront the psychological costs it exacts. Financial mastery requires not simply delegating tasks to machines, but cultivating a vigilant, reflective relationship with money—one that honours the complexities of human behaviour and the subtleties of intention. In acknowledging this, we move toward budgeting as a deliberate, conscious act, reclaiming sovereignty over the rhythms of spending in a world increasingly designed to make us forget.

The shift from budgeting as a deliberate act to an automated process mirrors broader societal trends, where passive consumption often replaces mindful participation. Yet, the stakes here are uniquely intimate: the erosion of financial agency impacts not just bank balances, but personal identity, future security, and emotional well-being. By unpacking the myth of control and exposing the psychological vulnerabilities embedded in "set it and forget it," we illuminate a path back to financial clarity—one grounded in awareness, choice, and responsibility. This understanding is foundational to resisting the quiet erosion of autonomy that subscription culture perpetuates and serves as the essential first step in reclaiming control over both money and mind.

When Spending Becomes Invisible

When spending becomes invisible, it ceases to register as a deliberate act and instead morphs into a silent drain on both financial resources and cognitive awareness. This phenomenon—best described as *monetary anesthesia*—captures a growing predicament in consumer behaviour, where recurring transactions lose their psychological impact, allowing costs to accumulate unnoticed and unchecked. This loss of price salience is not merely a quirk of modern payment technology but a systemic vulnerability exploited by subscription-based business models. Understanding the mechanisms behind this invisibility, and its tangible consequences, is essential for reclaiming financial agency in a world designed to make us forget.

Consider the story of Mark, a mid-career professional who, over several years, subscribed to a range of digital services: music streaming, meal kits, premium news outlets, online fitness classes, and more. Each subscription, priced modestly on its own, seemed justifiable at the moment of signup. Yet, over time, Mark ceased to use many of these services, too busy or disinterested to cancel. Because payments were automatically deducted each month, the expenses blended into the background noise of his finances. It was only when a major life event forced him to review his bank statements closely that he discovered he was losing over £300 monthly to subscriptions he barely remembered. Multiply this by twelve, and the annual loss is close to £4,000—a sum that could have been redirected to savings, debt reduction, or other priorities. Mark's experience is far from unique; such cases have become alarmingly common, highlighting the cognitive disconnect between spending and awareness inherent in subscription economies.

The root of this disconnection lies in the brain's response to financial transactions. Research in behavioural economics and cognitive psychology reveals that humans are highly sensitive to spending when it is tangible and immediate. The act of handing over cash or physically swiping a card engages neural pathways associated with pain and loss, prompting a cautious approach to spending. By contrast, automated payments—withdrawn silently and without direct involvement—fail to trigger these signals. This reduced salience dulls the emotional and cognitive weight of spending, making it easier to overlook or rationalise ongoing expenses. The term *monetary anesthesia* aptly describes this numbing effect, whereby repeated, low-salience payments erode the psychological brakes that typically regulate consumption.

This phenomenon is not merely theoretical; it has real-world implications that can significantly undermine personal finances. A study published in the *Journal of Consumer Research* found that consumers who paid with credit cards, rather than cash, were more likely to underestimate their spending and carry higher debt balances. When extended to the recurring payment model, the effect intensifies, because there is no discrete payment moment that demands conscious approval. Subscriptions convert what was once episodic spending into a continuous flow, further reducing the likelihood of cognitive engagement. The cumulative effect is a form of financial invisibility where money leaves accounts without commensurate awareness or control.

Businesses have capitalised on this invisibility by designing subscription models that reduce friction at signup and streamline automatic renewals, creating a "set it and forget it" environment that maximises customer retention. However, this convenience often masks a troubling asymmetry of information and effort. While customers must actively review, remember, and cancel services they no longer use, companies deploy user experience strategies that make cancellation difficult, counterintuitive, or time-consuming. This imbalance exploits well-documented psychological biases, including status quo bias and loss aversion, which incline individuals to maintain the default option—automatic payment—even when it no longer serves their interests. Such design strategies intentionally leverage the opacity and inertia created by monetary anesthesia, converting passive consumers into perpetual revenue streams.

At a cultural level, the ubiquity of invisible spending reshapes how individuals relate to money and value. Historically, the act of paying was an event—an occasion to reflect on choices and priorities. Today, the seamlessness of subscription payments divorces consumption from conscious evaluation, eroding the mental accounting practices that help consumers maintain budgets and align spending with values. This shift has implications beyond personal finance, touching on consumer autonomy and ethical consumption. When spending becomes unconscious, accountability weakens. Individuals may find themselves supporting services or companies misaligned with their principles simply because those payments escape their attention.

Some argue that automation is an inevitable adaptation to modern complexity, freeing consumers from tedious financial micromanagement and allowing them to focus on higher priorities. There is truth to this: reducing cognitive load is a legitimate goal, and many benefit from the reliability and convenience that autopay provides. Yet the critical question is where to draw the line between helpful automation and dangerous disengagement. Without deliberate strategies to maintain visibility—such as regular financial reviews or subscription audits—automation risks undermining the very control it promises. It becomes a double-edged sword, substituting ease for oversight, and convenience for consciousness.

Real-world examples illustrate the stakes involved. Sarah, a university lecturer, found that over five years, her subscriptions to educational platforms, wellness apps, and digital magazines cost her nearly £2,500 annually. Many were no longer relevant to her current needs but persisted because cancellation processes were buried behind labyrinthine menus or delayed customer support. Similarly, Tom, a freelance graphic designer, discovered that bundled software subscriptions he had trialled during a project continued to auto-renew long after completion, quietly eroding his tight budget. These cases demonstrate how monetary anesthesia, combined with systemic design choices, can translate into significant financial leakage that compounds silently over time.

The psychological dimensions of this issue are critical to understand. Monetary anesthesia exploits fundamental features of human cognition: our limited attention spans, tendency toward cognitive overload, and preference for minimal effort. By rendering spending invisible, subscription models tap into these vulnerabilities, creating a feedback loop where diminished awareness begets further disengagement. Breaking this loop requires both awareness and structural change—tools and habits that restore the salience of spending and encourage active financial stewardship. It also demands a critical examination of how technology shapes behaviour and where ethical boundaries should be drawn in service design.

Ethical considerations come sharply into focus when considering the balance between business interests and consumer welfare. The strategic opacity of subscription renewals and cancellation processes raises questions about informed consent and fair practice. Regulators in several jurisdictions have begun to address these issues, implementing rules requiring clearer disclosures and easier cancellation mechanisms. Yet much of the onus remains on consumers to educate themselves and proactively manage their financial relationships. This imbalance underscores the necessity for cultural shifts that prioritise financial literacy and empower consumers to reclaim visibility over their spending.

To counteract monetary anesthesia, several practical measures have demonstrated efficacy. Financial technology innovations now offer subscription-tracking tools that aggregate recurring charges and alert users to unused services. Integrating these tools with regular budgeting routines helps reinstate conscious engagement. Moreover, adopting a habit of periodic 'subscription audits'—meticulously reviewing bank statements and app accounts—can illuminate hidden drains and prompt timely cancellations. Perhaps most importantly, cultivating a mindset that views each transaction as an opportunity for reflection rather than a mere procedural event restores the psychological salience critical to financial health.

The invisibility of spending through subscriptions is not merely a technical issue but a challenge to autonomy and self-awareness. It reflects a broader tension in contemporary consumer culture between convenience and control, efficiency and mindfulness. As subscription models proliferate and payments become ever more seamless, the imperative to resist monetary anesthesia grows more urgent. By recognising and confronting this phenomenon, individuals can begin to reclaim clarity and intention in their financial lives, transforming budgeting from an automated routine into a conscious practice of stewardship.

This exploration reveals that invisibility in spending is not an incidental by-product of digital finance but a core dynamic engineered into the system. It challenges readers to question the assumptions underlying convenience and to critically examine the psychological mechanisms that govern their financial behaviours. Engaging with these issues lays the groundwork for resisting the silent erosion of resources and awareness, fostering a renewed relationship with money that is both vigilant and intentional. In doing so, we move toward a financial culture that honours the intricate interplay between cognition, emotion, and economic agency—one where spending is visible, meaningful, and aligned with the values we choose to uphold.

From Ownership to Access

The transition from owning to accessing goods and services represents one of the most significant economic and cultural shifts of recent decades. At first glance, the subscription economy promises unprecedented convenience, flexibility, and affordability. Instead of investing large sums to own a product outright, consumers now pay smaller, ongoing fees to access services or items on demand. Yet beneath this surface appeal lies a complex transformation that challenges long-standing assumptions about possession, value, and identity. What do we truly lose when permanence yields to perpetual rental? The shift from ownership to access reshapes not only financial relationships but also cognitive frameworks and cultural norms in ways that demand careful scrutiny.

Ownership has historically conferred more than legal title; it anchored individual and collective identity, provided a sense of control, and fostered a deep connection to possessions. Psychologists and anthropologists have long observed that humans form attachments to objects they own, imbuing them with meaning beyond mere utility. A book on one's shelf, a photograph on a wall, or a car parked in the driveway serve as extensions of self, markers of status, memory, and aspiration. Ownership creates permanence—a stable reference point in a changing world that supports planning, pride, and responsibility. Philosophically, it reinforces notions of autonomy and agency; owning something implies mastery over that object, and by extension, a measure of control over one's environment.

The rise of subscription models, by contrast, privileges access over possession. Whether it is streaming music, software services, clothing rentals, or even transportation, consumers increasingly pay for temporary use without acquiring lasting rights. This *shift to access* promises flexibility and lower upfront costs, appealing especially to younger generations whose lifestyles emphasise mobility and immediacy. For many, subscribing removes burdens associated with maintenance, depreciation, and disposal. Yet, this convenience is accompanied by a subtle erosion of permanence, disrupting the cognitive and emotional scaffolding that ownership provides.

Financially, the implications are profound. Ownership implies an asset that retains some residual value or can be leveraged as collateral, contributing to wealth accumulation and economic stability. Renting or subscribing, however, converts what was once a capital expense into an operational expense—a recurring cost that never culminates in equity. While this can improve cash flow management and reduce barriers to entry, it often obscures the long-term financial trajectory. Over time, the cumulative expense of perpetual rental can exceed the cost of outright purchase, a phenomenon frequently overlooked amid the allure of lower monthly payments. Moreover, the absence of ownership restricts consumers' options: they cannot modify, resell, or pass on the service or product, limiting their agency and economic flexibility.

Consider the example of the automotive industry, where the emergence of subscription services for cars—allowing drivers to switch vehicles monthly—embodies this trend vividly. For consumers, this offers unparalleled choice and eliminates concerns about depreciation or long-term commitment. Yet, this model also detaches the user from the concept of personal vehicle ownership, which traditionally confers not only practical utility but a psychological sense of independence and identity. Owning a car has long symbolised freedom and status; subscribing transforms it into a transient experience, contingent on ongoing payments and corporate policies. For some, this shift signals liberation from burdensome responsibilities; for others, a loss of control and permanence.

Cognitively, the move from ownership to access reconfigures how individuals process value and relate to material culture. Ownership demands deliberation and commitment; purchasing a good entails research, evaluation, and anticipation of future use. Access, especially when facilitated by frictionless subscription interfaces, encourages consumption that is transient, flexible, and often impulsive. This can dilute the perceived value of goods and services, as their temporary nature diminishes emotional investment. The psychological attachment that ownership fosters is replaced by a more fleeting engagement, where disposability and replaceability become norms. This shift challenges established behavioural economics models that link ownership to more cautious and thoughtful consumption patterns.

Culturally, the implications extend beyond individual psychology to shape social norms and expectations. Ownership has traditionally structured economic and social relations, from property rights to inheritance to community belonging. As access supplants ownership, societies confront new questions about equity, security, and responsibility. For instance, when digital goods, knowledge, or even housing become primarily accessible through subscription or rental arrangements, the stability once guaranteed by ownership rights diminishes. This raises concerns about long-term security and autonomy, especially for vulnerable populations whose access may be subject to disruption by economic shifts or corporate decisions. The erosion of ownership rights potentially deepens precarity, fostering dependence on external providers rather than fostering self-determination.

These tensions are palpable in the domain of digital media. The shift from owning physical books, CDs, or DVDs to subscribing to digital platforms reflects a broader cultural realignment. While access provides unparalleled convenience and breadth of choice, it also means that consumers do not possess permanent copies of cultural artefacts. Content libraries can change, disappear, or be subject to geo-restrictions, stripping consumers of control once taken for granted. The loss of permanence here is not merely practical but symbolic, challenging notions of cultural stewardship and individual agency in shaping one's intellectual and aesthetic environment.

Opposing views suggest that the move to access may democratise consumption and reduce waste. By sharing resources and enabling more efficient use, subscription models could promote sustainability and social inclusion. For example, clothing rental services can reduce the environmental impact of fast fashion by encouraging reuse. Car-sharing schemes can lower emissions by reducing the need for individual ownership. These benefits illustrate that the shift from ownership to access is not unambiguously detrimental but complex and multifaceted. It invites a reassessment of what value means in contemporary economies, balancing permanence with adaptability, possession with flexibility.

Nevertheless, critical scrutiny reveals that the pervasive narrative of "access is better" often masks economic and psychological costs. The perpetual rental model risks commodifying everyday life in ways that undermine autonomy and deepen consumer dependence. The absence of permanence erodes cognitive anchors that help individuals organise their financial and emotional lives, complicating efforts to plan for the future or assert control over personal wealth. This dislocation can foster feelings of rootlessness and dissatisfaction, as the intangible nature of access fails to satisfy deeper human needs for stability and meaningful connection.

To navigate this complex landscape, consumers and policymakers alike must cultivate a nuanced understanding of the trade-offs involved. Financial literacy education should incorporate awareness of subscription economics and the implications of renting versus owning. Individuals can benefit from reflecting on their own values and priorities, discerning when access enhances flexibility and when ownership better supports long-term goals. Policymakers face the challenge of ensuring that legal frameworks protect consumer rights in an economy where property boundaries blur and control becomes diffuse.

In sum, the shift from ownership to access is neither a straightforward improvement nor a regress; it is a profound transformation with layered consequences. It redefines relationships with materiality, challenges cognitive models of value and control, and reshapes cultural norms about permanence and agency. Recognising what is lost—and gained—in this transition equips us to engage more critically and consciously with the subscription economy. It opens space for a reimagined financial culture that honours both flexibility and stability, embracing access where it serves autonomy while preserving ownership where it cultivates identity, responsibility, and security.

The Convenience Tradeoff

The promise of convenience has become the defining allure of modern technology, shaping how we live, work, and consume. It is the magic ingredient in every app, platform, and service—one that claims to save time, reduce friction, and simplify complex decisions. Yet, beneath this seductive surface lies a more troubling reality: the convenience engineered into digital ecosystems is often weaponised to bypass our financial decision-making processes, transforming convenience into a mechanism of control and extraction. This convenience tradeoff demands critical scrutiny because what appears as ease and efficiency frequently carries hidden costs—eroding autonomy, blurring boundaries of consent, and draining both attention and capital with minimal resistance.

At first glance, the digital economy's obsession with seamless user experience (UX) seems an unqualified benefit. Why wouldn't we want to reduce clicks, eliminate forms, and make payments as effortless as a tap or a voice command? The logic is compelling: frictionless interfaces reduce cognitive load, increase satisfaction, and democratise access to services that once required substantial time and effort. Take Amazon's "one-click" ordering, which revolutionised online shopping by eliminating barriers to purchase, or Spotify's instant streaming that grants access to millions of songs without download or ownership. These innovations have undeniably reshaped consumer behaviour, making access smoother and faster than ever before.

However, this very ease that delights users also short-circuits the psychological safeguards that traditionally govern spending decisions. Behavioural economists have long demonstrated that friction—those small hurdles in a transaction—is essential in promoting deliberation and reducing impulsive behaviour. When friction is removed, the brain's critical evaluative mechanisms often fail to activate. A study in *Psychological Science* found that even minimal increases in purchase difficulty significantly reduce impulsive buying. Conversely, reducing effort and increasing immediacy amplifies automatic, often less reflective spending. Modern UX design exploits this by crafting experiences where subscription sign-ups, renewals, and upsells unfold without deliberate confirmation, slipping past conscious scrutiny.

A revealing example comes from the world of mobile gaming, where microtransactions exemplify frictionless monetisation. Games often employ "paywalls" that gently nudge players towards spending real money to bypass delays or acquire advantages. Payment prompts are designed to be quick and effortless, with saved card details and in-app wallets enabling immediate purchase. Players, often immersed and emotionally engaged, may spend more than intended precisely because the interface eliminates traditional cognitive checks. This engineered ease transforms spending from a considered choice into a reflexive habit, a phenomenon sometimes called "dark patterns" in UX—design elements that manipulate users into actions beneficial to the provider but potentially detrimental to the user.

Subscription services, too, wield frictionless UX to entrench revenue streams. The signup process is streamlined to encourage enrolment, often accompanied by free trials that require credit card details upfront. While users can ostensibly cancel at any time, the cancellation process itself is frequently riddled with friction: hidden menus, multi-step confirmations, and delayed customer service responses. This asymmetry creates a retention bias, where the effort to remain subscribed is trivial, but the effort to exit is substantial. The result is a behavioural lock-in reinforced by inertia, where consumers unknowingly sustain payments for unused or unwanted services. This dynamic exemplifies how convenience for acquisition contrasts sharply with complexity in cancellation, a deliberate tactic that capitalises on human tendencies toward procrastination and avoidance.

Financial decision-making circuits are further compromised by continuous, invisible payments. Automatic renewals reduce the salience of spending because they require no active authorisation. When money departs silently, without immediate action or physical exchange, it becomes cognitively dissociated from consumption. This "monetary anesthesia" undermines the brain's capacity to track expenses accurately, facilitating unchecked accumulation of costs. The frictionless UX designed to maximise ease thus paradoxically facilitates a disengagement from the very financial stewardship consumers assume they maintain. The convenience tradeoff reveals itself here as a subtle erosion of autonomy cloaked in seamless interaction.

Critically, the costs of convenience extend beyond individual finances to affect broader societal and ethical domains. By engineering interfaces that prioritise retention and spend over informed consent, companies commodify attention and exploit behavioural vulnerabilities. This raises urgent questions about the moral responsibilities of tech firms and the need for regulatory frameworks that protect consumers from manipulative design. The

European Union's recent Digital Services Act and Consumer Rights Directive reflect emerging efforts to address these concerns by mandating clearer information, easier cancellations, and protections against dark patterns. Yet legislative responses often lag behind rapidly evolving technologies, underscoring the importance of consumer awareness and digital literacy as frontline defences.

Despite these challenges, convenience need not be an unmitigated threat. Thoughtfully designed friction can coexist with user-friendly interfaces to promote autonomy and informed choice. For example, some platforms have begun introducing deliberate "pause" options for subscriptions, transparent summaries of recurring charges, and proactive reminders before renewals. These features restore moments of reflection without sacrificing overall usability. The emerging field of ethical UX design advocates for such balanced approaches, arguing that respect for user agency and transparency should guide innovation as much as profit maximisation.

Consumers themselves can adopt strategies to navigate the convenience tradeoff more effectively. Regular financial audits that focus specifically on subscriptions and automatic payments help illuminate hidden drains. Utilising apps designed to monitor recurring charges and prompt timely cancellations can restore visibility. Perhaps most importantly, cultivating a mindset that treats convenience with cautious respect—embracing its benefits but questioning its costs—empowers individuals to regain control. This involves recognising when seamless interfaces serve our goals and when they serve corporate interests that may diverge from our own.

The convenience tradeoff embodies a fundamental tension in the digital economy: the desire for effortless access colliding with the necessity of deliberate stewardship. As technology relentlessly pursues ever smoother, faster, and more intuitive interactions, consumers must remain vigilant against the erosion of their financial and cognitive sovereignty. The veneer of ease conceals mechanisms designed to capture attention, minimise resistance, and perpetuate spending patterns that often go unexamined. By deconstructing these hidden costs and understanding how frictionless UX functions as a tool of behavioural influence, we reclaim the possibility of intentional, conscious engagement with our money. This reclamation is not a rejection of convenience but an invitation to wield it wisely—balancing the promises of modern technology with the timeless demands of self-awareness and agency.

Chapter 2
Cognitive Hazards of the Subscription Mindset

In the quieter recesses of our financial lives, subtle psychological forces operate almost invisibly, shaping how we relate to the steady, almost hypnotic rhythm of subscription payments. What seems innocuous—a small monthly charge here, another there—conceals a lattice of cognitive tendencies and emotional attachments that can turn money management into something less deliberate, more automatic, and at times strangely irrational. This chapter probes those undercurrents, showing how the subscription model exploits natural quirks of memory, habit, and identity, ensnaring even the most careful of spenders in patterns that feel benign but accumulate with surprising weight.

Consider, first, the forgetting curve of money. Neuroscientists remind us that routine experiences, particularly those without strong emotional resonance, slip rapidly from memory unless we actively pay attention. Recurring charges are almost engineered to capitalise on this trait: seamless, repetitive, and designed to pass under the radar. A one-off purchase prompts reflection—do I want this? Can I afford it?—whereas the monthly debit, quietly processed, rarely sets off the alarm bells of budgetary oversight. Over time, this cognitive blind spot becomes fertile ground for financial leakage. Yet there is a silver lining. Awareness of the pattern itself invites an act of reclamation: combing through bank statements not as dreary admin, but as a mindful encounter with the flow of one's money, a reassertion of presence where automation prefers absence.

Entwined with forgetfulness is another trap: the allure of microcommitments. A few pounds a month feels trivial, almost laughably small—so small that declining seems pedantic. And yet, string a dozen such charges together, let them roll over for a handful of years, and the cumulative cost becomes anything but negligible. Behavioural economics has long warned of our difficulty in grasping compounding effects, and here the mismatch between perception and reality is stark. The subscription economy thrives on this gap, inviting us to focus on the apparent affordability of the present while quietly binding us to long-term obligations. The paradox is familiar: what feels like freedom—flexibility, low cost—often hardens into constraint.

But these snares are not only cognitive; they are emotional, even existential. The sunk cost fallacy exerts its pull: "I've already paid for this, so I might as well keep going." Layered upon this is identity itself. We cling to certain subscriptions not because we use them, but because they reinforce a narrative: I'm the sort of person who listens to that service, takes that course, supports that platform. Cancelling, then, becomes more than financial housekeeping—it feels like a small betrayal of self-image. Here, money is woven into story, and the difficulty of letting go reveals just how deeply financial choices are embedded in our sense of who we are.

And then comes the mirage of personalisation. Algorithms, armed with oceans of data, present us with what seems like a tailored fit—recommendations that feel intimate, as though the platform understands us better than we know ourselves. This semblance of bespoke attention creates a peculiar bond: it flatters, it resonates, and in doing so, it justifies ongoing payment. Yet beneath the surface lies a commercial imperative, not a personal one: to maximise engagement, to elongate the lifetime of the subscription, to keep us tethered. The charm of relevance disguises the fact that the value delivered may be thinner, less essential, than the emotional tug suggests.

Taken together, these dynamics form a constellation of risks that reshape how we spend. Human minds, evolved for survival in environments of scarcity and immediacy, falter in the engineered abundance of the digital economy. We forget what recurs, underestimate what accrues, cling to what we've paid for, and overvalue what feels personal. Recognising this doesn't solve the problem outright, but it does provide a foothold. Each insight—about forgetfulness, about microcommitments, about sunk costs and algorithmic seductions—creates the possibility of stepping back, of seeing the trap before it snaps shut.

The argument here is not abstract. It draws upon findings from neuroscience, behavioural economics, psychology, and technology studies, grounding theory in lived reality. Stories abound of forgotten subscriptions draining accounts, of individuals carrying digital baggage simply because they once believed it mattered, of platforms that whisper relevance into our ears until the habit becomes reflex. Interspersed with these examples are invitations to pause, to turn awareness into practice: to review, to question, to test whether what we pay for still serves us.

The subscription mindset, then, is not merely a financial model but a psychological environment. It blurs the line between convenience and complacency, between identity and expenditure, between autonomy and algorithmic design. To navigate it requires a framework that acknowledges these entanglements, not just in theory but in practice. That is the purpose of this chapter: to lay bare the hidden scaffolding of subscription spending, so that readers can approach their financial lives with greater clarity and, crucially, with intention.

So, as you move forward, consider not just the services you subscribe to but the meanings you attach to them. Ask whether each charge is a tool or a tether, a conscious choice or an unnoticed drift. In doing so, you reclaim what the subscription economy would prefer you relinquish: the ability to act with awareness, to choose rather than default, and to let your financial habits reflect not manipulation but mindful autonomy.

The Forgetting Curve of Money

The human brain is a marvel of adaptability, constantly prioritising information to focus on what matters most in the moment. Yet, this incredible efficiency comes with a trade-off: the natural tendency to forget routine, low-salience details. When applied to money, this cognitive quirk becomes what can be termed the *forgetting curve of money*—a neurological and behavioural phenomenon whereby routine financial transactions, especially those that require little effort or conscious engagement, fade quickly from memory. This innate forgetfulness is not merely an incidental feature of human cognition; it is a vulnerability that modern technology and subscription models exploit systematically, allowing small but persistent charges to slip under the radar of awareness and accumulate into significant financial burdens.

Neuroscientific research has long established that memory retention declines exponentially unless reinforced by repetition, emotional significance, or active recall. Hermann Ebbinghaus's seminal work on the forgetting curve demonstrated that without such reinforcement, individuals forget approximately half of newly acquired information within an hour, and up to 90% within a month. While Ebbinghaus studied verbal material, the principles apply broadly, including to how we register financial transactions. Spending that is automatic, repetitive, and low in immediate consequence is precisely the kind of experience that the brain deems unworthy of encoding into long-term memory. This neurological filtering conserves cognitive resources but leaves consumers susceptible to what behavioural economists call "payment decoupling"—a disconnect between the act of paying and the psychological impact of spending.

To appreciate the implications, consider the contrasting experiences of two types of payments. A one-off purchase, such as buying a laptop or a holiday, commands attention because it is infrequent, significant in amount, and involves active decision-making. The brain registers this as a salient event, fostering emotional engagement and memory formation. On the other hand, a monthly subscription to a music streaming service or a cloud storage plan often involves minimal cognitive effort: the amount is small, the payment is automatic, and it recurs with monotonous regularity. These characteristics mute the mental "pain" of spending, making it easier to overlook or rationalise. Over time, this repeated invisibility fosters *monetary anesthesia*, where the brain's alert systems disengage, undermining financial vigilance.

The technology ecosystem has evolved to capitalise on this cognitive blind spot. Subscription services deliberately design billing systems to be as seamless and frictionless as possible, minimising notifications and requiring no active authorisation after initial enrolment. Features like saved payment details, automatic renewals, and silent deductions encourage a passive relationship with money that sidesteps the brain's natural mechanisms for oversight. This architectural invisibility is a strategic design choice: the less effort a consumer exerts to notice or approve charges, the higher the likelihood of sustained revenue streams. A striking example comes from the streaming media industry, where studies have found that consumers often continue to pay for multiple platforms simultaneously, even when actively using only one or none. The cognitive ease of ignoring these recurring payments masks their aggregate cost, which can reach several hundred pounds a year unnoticed.

Real-world cases illustrate how this forgetting curve manifests with tangible consequences. Take Lucy, a marketing executive who subscribed to various wellness apps during periods of stress, each costing around £10 monthly. Initially valuable, many fell into disuse as her circumstances changed. Without active tracking, these payments accumulated invisibly for years. When Lucy finally audited her finances, she was shocked to discover over £1,200 had been spent on dormant subscriptions. Her experience is echoed in consumer reports and financial advisory studies, which reveal that a significant proportion of people unknowingly pay for unused or forgotten services. This systemic leakage is not merely a personal oversight but a widespread pattern fuelled by human cognitive limitations and deliberate design.

The forgetting curve also interacts with behavioural economics concepts such as *mental accounting*—the mental categorisation of money into discrete budgets or purposes. Recurring payments often occupy a separate mental compartment labelled "subscriptions" or "utilities," perceived as fixed or unavoidable. This categorisation discourages active scrutiny, as these charges are mentally compartmentalised away from discretionary spending. Yet, their cumulative effect can distort overall budgetary control. The challenge lies in bridging this cognitive gap by reintegrating automatic payments into conscious financial management.

Addressing the forgetting curve of money requires more than passive hope that individuals will spontaneously remember their expenditures. Instead, it calls for deliberate strategies to counteract natural memory decay and restore financial awareness. One effective approach is the *reflection exercise*—a systematic audit of bank statements and payment histories focused explicitly on identifying forgotten or ignored charges. This exercise transforms memory from a passive faculty into an active practice of financial mindfulness. By dedicating time to review every recurring payment, readers confront the often surprising reality of their subscription landscape, disrupting the invisibility cloak woven by automation.

The reflection exercise can be structured as follows: begin by collecting all recent bank and credit card statements spanning at least six months. Catalogue every recurring payment, noting the service, amount, frequency, and date of the last interaction or usage. For each subscription, ask probing questions: Do I still use this service regularly? Does it provide sufficient value to justify its cost? Could I pause or cancel it without detriment? This process not only surfaces forgotten expenses but also encourages evaluative thinking, bridging the gap between automatic payments and conscious choice. Over time, integrating this audit into regular budgeting routines helps counteract the neurological tendency to forget.

It is important to recognise that this cognitive vulnerability is not a flaw in individuals but a mismatch between evolved human memory systems and contemporary financial technologies. Historically, spending was a tactile, episodic event, often involving physical currency and face-to-face transactions that left strong cognitive traces. The rise of digital payments and subscription models has outpaced the brain's ability to adapt instantaneously, creating a systemic gap. This misalignment calls for new forms of financial literacy and technological innovation that prioritise visibility and user control. For instance, financial management apps that consolidate subscription data and provide timely alerts can act as cognitive prosthetics, supplementing human memory and promoting proactive oversight.

Critics might argue that constant vigilance over small recurring charges imposes undue cognitive load and detracts from the convenience and efficiency digital finance offers. This perspective has merit; cognitive resources are finite, and over-monitoring risks decision fatigue. The solution lies not in abolishing automation but in striking a balance—leveraging technology's efficiency while embedding mechanisms that periodically restore conscious engagement. Thoughtful design that incorporates reminder systems, transparent billing, and user-friendly cancellation processes can mitigate the risks posed by monetary anesthesia without sacrificing usability.

Moreover, recognising the forgetting curve as a fundamental cognitive constraint invites ethical reflection on the responsibilities of businesses and regulators. The deliberate minimisation of payment salience raises questions about informed consent and consumer protection. Regulatory frameworks in some jurisdictions have begun to address these issues, mandating clearer disclosures and more accessible cancellation options. Yet, much depends on consumers cultivating habits and tools that counterbalance systemic opacity. Empowerment emerges through a combination of awareness, technological aids, and supportive policy.

The forgetting curve of money thus encapsulates a critical intersection of neuroscience, behavioural economics, technology design, and ethics. It challenges the prevailing assumption that financial control is merely a matter of willpower or discipline, instead highlighting how unconscious cognitive processes shape spending patterns. Understanding this phenomenon equips readers to approach their financial lives with humility and strategy, acknowledging natural limitations while harnessing reflection and technology to reclaim agency.

As you consider your own financial habits, this chapter invites you to engage actively with the invisible flows of money that permeate your life. The reflection exercise is more than a practical tool—it is a deliberate act of remembering, an antidote to the cognitive forces that seek to render spending invisible. Through this process, budgeting evolves from a reactive checklist into a mindful practice, reconnecting you with your money and the choices it represents. This foundation is essential for navigating the subscription economy thoughtfully, transforming forgetfulness from a vulnerability into an opportunity for clarity and control.

The Allure of Microcommitments

The lure of microcommitments—the seemingly trivial, low-cost subscriptions that permeate modern consumer culture—has quietly reshaped our financial landscape. What appears as modest monthly fees, often less than the cost of a coffee, aggregate into substantial long-term expenses that many fail to fully grasp. This "small now, big later" paradox exploits cognitive biases and behavioural economics principles, revealing how incremental spending can culminate in significant financial drain. Understanding the allure of microcommitments is crucial for anyone seeking to navigate the subscription economy with clarity and control, as it exposes the subtle mechanisms by which convenience and affordability can mask cumulative cost.

At the core of this paradox lies the psychological concept of *transaction utility*, which suggests that consumers derive satisfaction not only from the product or service itself but from the perceived deal or price fairness. Small payments feel manageable and low-risk, triggering a positive emotional response that lowers spending resistance. When a subscription costs just a few pounds per month, it registers as an affordable indulgence rather than a significant expenditure. This perception is reinforced by the recurring nature of subscriptions, which distribute costs evenly over time, diluting the immediate financial impact. The human brain, attuned to respond to lump sums more than to diffuse, repeated charges, often underestimates the aggregate cost, falling prey to a cognitive disconnect between present perception and future reality.

This phenomenon is well documented in behavioural economics, where the *mental accounting* framework explains how individuals compartmentalise expenses, treating small recurring fees differently from larger one-off payments. Unlike a £120 annual fee paid upfront, a £10 monthly charge feels less urgent and is more easily integrated into day-to-day spending categories, often without rigorous scrutiny. This mental partitioning shields consumers from the cumulative effect, allowing multiple micro-subscriptions to coexist unnoticed within budgets. Yet, when aggregated, these small amounts can rival or exceed traditional larger expenses, quietly eroding disposable income and saving potential.

Real-world examples illuminate this dynamic. For instance, a 2021 consumer survey found that the average UK household subscribed to more than four digital services simultaneously, with many unaware of the full extent of recurring payments. Individuals like James, a graphic designer, initially subscribed to a range of creative software, online courses, and entertainment platforms, each costing less than £15 a month. Over time, as his interests shifted and some services fell into disuse, he failed to cancel them. After a financial review prompted by unexpected bills, James realised he was paying nearly £600 annually for underutilised subscriptions. The incremental nature of these payments had obscured their total impact, exemplifying the "small now, big later" effect.

The subscription model itself incentivises this spending pattern by lowering psychological barriers to entry. Free trials, introductory offers, and tiered pricing encourage consumers to commit incrementally, with the hope that ease and habituation will cement long-term retention. This tactic capitalises on the *foot-in-the-door* effect, a social psychology principle where agreeing to a small request increases the likelihood of consenting to larger demands later. Once accustomed to the service, consumers find cancellation effortful or dissonant, while the monthly cost feels too insignificant to warrant action. This dynamic fosters a cycle where microcommitments multiply, often unchecked.

Yet, the allure of microcommitments extends beyond cognitive biases into the realm of emotional and social psychology. Many subscriptions serve not only functional purposes but also contribute to identity and lifestyle signalling. Being a member of a niche streaming platform, a specialised fitness app, or a curated book club confers a sense of belonging or personal enrichment. These subscriptions become part of a self-narrative, reinforcing identity through repeated expenditure. This intertwining of consumption with self-concept complicates decisions to cancel, as microcommitments accrue emotional as well as financial weight.

Despite these challenges, recognising the paradox is the first step towards mitigation. Thoughtful budgeting practices that account for cumulative subscription costs enable consumers to regain perspective. Regular audits of recurring payments—mapping them against usage and value—can illuminate overlooked drains and prompt informed decisions. Digital tools and apps designed for subscription tracking have emerged as valuable allies, translating dispersed micro-payments into coherent overviews that confront the illusion of insignificance. Moreover, cultivating an evaluative mindset that weighs long-term financial impact against short-term convenience disrupts the default acceptance of microcommitments.

Critically, the subscription economy's reliance on microcommitments raises broader ethical and systemic questions. While offering accessibility and flexibility, these models often prioritise revenue growth over consumer well-being, exploiting cognitive blind spots for profit. The diffuse, incremental nature of spending can obscure transparency, complicating consumers' ability to make fully informed choices. Regulatory interventions focusing on clearer disclosures, simplified cancellation processes, and spending caps may help address these concerns, but ultimately, consumer education and empowerment remain essential.

In reflecting on the "small now, big later" paradox, it becomes evident that microcommitments represent a profound shift in how we experience and manage financial obligations. They transform spending into a continuous, low-friction stream that can easily escape scrutiny, challenging traditional budgeting frameworks. Navigating this landscape requires a blend of awareness, technological support, and behavioural discipline. By engaging critically with the allure of microcommitments, readers can reclaim financial clarity, turning what once seemed negligible into manageable, intentional choices. This insight is indispensable for thriving in the subscription economy—where the real cost is often hidden in plain sight.

Sunk Cost & Identity Traps

Human beings are storytellers by nature, weaving narratives that define who they are and how they see the world. These narratives extend deeply into the realm of consumption, where what we buy, use, or subscribe to often becomes intertwined with our identity. Nowhere is this more evident—and potentially problematic—than in the psychology behind why many individuals persist with subscriptions that no longer serve their interests or needs. This persistence is frequently anchored in two powerful cognitive phenomena: the sunk cost fallacy and identity attachment. Together, they create a compelling psychological trap that sustains spending long after its rational justification has evaporated.

The sunk cost fallacy refers to the tendency to continue investing in a decision based on the irrecoverable costs already incurred, rather than on the current and future value of that decision. In subscription contexts, this might look like maintaining an underused membership because of the money already spent, even when the service no longer provides meaningful benefit. The logic is flawed but psychologically potent: people feel compelled to justify past expenditures, fearing that cancellation would signify a loss or failure. This creates a powerful inertia that resists change, effectively turning subscriptions into financial deadweight. Such commitment is rarely a product of conscious reasoning; rather, it is an unconscious defence mechanism aimed at preserving self-consistency and avoiding regret.

Closely intertwined with this is the concept of identity attachment—how subscriptions become embedded in personal and social identity. Consider the assertion, "I'm the kind of person who has MasterClass," or "I subscribe to that because it fits my lifestyle." These statements reveal that subscriptions are more than services; they are symbols that convey who we are or aspire to be. This identity-based commitment often prevents individuals from cancelling subscriptions even when usage declines or costs become burdensome. The subscription transcends its material function and becomes a psychological anchor, affirming values, ambitions, or social belonging. Disentangling oneself from these attachments can feel like a threat to the coherence of self, explaining why many tolerate financial inefficiency to preserve identity narratives.

These phenomena are not abstract concepts but deeply embodied experiences with clear financial consequences. Take Sarah, a professional who subscribed to a suite of online learning platforms early in her career. Over time, her priorities shifted, and she rarely engaged with these services. However, she continued paying for them, partly because she identified as a lifelong learner and felt that cancelling would contradict that self-image. Simultaneously, she justified the ongoing cost by recalling the considerable investment already made. Sarah's story illustrates how sunk costs and identity attachment intertwine to create a potent subscription inertia, reflecting common patterns observed in behavioural finance research.

Neuroscientific studies support this understanding by demonstrating how the brain's reward and self-referential processing systems reinforce sunk cost and identity effects. The anterior cingulate cortex, implicated in conflict monitoring and decision-making, becomes active when individuals face choices that could invalidate past investments, generating discomfort that motivates persistence. Similarly, regions involved in self-representation engage when consumption choices align with identity, making dissonance avoidance a powerful behavioural driver. These neural underpinnings highlight why cancelling a subscription is rarely a neutral financial decision—it is often a psychologically charged act with implications for self-concept and emotional equilibrium.

This cognitive entanglement complicates straightforward economic models of consumer rationality. Traditional frameworks assume that individuals evaluate ongoing costs against benefits independently of past expenditures or identity factors. Yet, behavioural economics reveals that decisions are profoundly shaped by psychological context. The sunk cost fallacy biases individuals toward loss aversion, where the pain of admitting a past mistake outweighs the rational benefits of discontinuation. Identity attachment amplifies this by introducing social and emotional stakes. Together, they foster what might be called *subscription loyalty*, not grounded in actual utility but in psychological investment.

Acknowledging these dynamics is critical for developing effective strategies to overcome subscription traps. Awareness of sunk cost bias empowers consumers to reframe their perspective, recognising that past payments are irretrievable and should not dictate current choices. Practically, this might involve exercises that separate historical spending from future decisions, such as imagining evaluating subscriptions as if for the first time. Addressing identity attachment requires more nuanced reflection. Individuals must explore the symbolic meanings they assign to subscriptions and consider alternative ways to affirm those identities without financial cost. For example, embracing a learner identity might shift from paid memberships to free community resources or personal projects.

The market and technology environment further complicate these psychological hurdles. Subscription platforms often encourage identity reinforcement through personalised content, badges, or social features that deepen engagement. This can strengthen emotional bonds, making cancellation psychologically costly beyond the monetary expense. Moreover, marketing strategies frequently frame subscriptions as essential components of aspirational lifestyles, embedding them in broader cultural narratives. Recognising these external influences aids consumers in distinguishing authentic personal values from constructed commercial identities.

Critically, this analysis invites ethical reflection on the responsibilities of subscription providers. Designing services that exploit sunk cost and identity attachments without transparency raises questions about consumer autonomy and fairness. While fostering loyalty is a legitimate business goal, the deliberate cultivation of psychological dependency risks crossing into manipulation. Regulatory attention to clear cancellation policies, transparent communication, and consumer education can help mitigate these risks, promoting more equitable market relationships.

In sum, the sunk cost and identity traps reveal the intricate psychological machinery that underlies many subscription decisions. They expose why financial rationality often yields to emotional and cognitive biases, entangling consumers in ongoing commitments that no longer serve them. By illuminating these mechanisms, this chapter equips readers to recognise their own vulnerabilities, disentangle identity from expenditure, and reclaim agency over their subscriptions. Understanding these traps is essential not only for individual financial health but for fostering a consumer culture that honours conscious choice over unconscious compulsion.

The Personalization Mirage

Algorithmic personalization—the process by which digital platforms tailor content, recommendations, and advertisements to individual users—has become a defining feature of the subscription economy. It promises a uniquely curated experience, one that seems designed to fit our tastes, needs, and aspirations like a bespoke garment. Yet beneath this allure lies what might be called the *personalization mirage*: a carefully constructed illusion of uniqueness that fosters emotional dependency and justifies ongoing spending, regardless of whether the perceived value is genuine or sustained. This mirage has profound implications for consumer autonomy, financial decision-making, and the very nature of value in the digital age.

At its core, personalization operates through sophisticated data collection and machine learning algorithms that analyse user behaviour—search histories, consumption patterns, preferences, and even subtle interactions—to predict and present content that appears relevant and timely. The psychological impact is potent. By creating an experience that feels tailored and intimate, platforms engage users not merely as consumers but as individuals whose identities and desires are understood and anticipated. This sense of being "seen" and catered to triggers emotional resonance, building loyalty and increasing the likelihood of sustained engagement and expenditure.

However, this perceived uniqueness is largely an engineered artefact rather than a reflection of authentic fit. Algorithms rely on patterns derived from large datasets, optimising for metrics such as time spent, click-through rates, and subscription retention. The content served is less about meeting genuine individual needs and more about maximising engagement and monetisation. This distinction is crucial: personalization is not inherently about enhancing user welfare but about driving commercial outcomes. The emotional attachment it fosters, therefore, can obscure the actual utility or value derived from the service, encouraging ongoing spend based on a curated narrative rather than an objective assessment.

The personalization mirage gains further traction through what behavioural scientists term *confirmation bias*—the tendency to favour information that confirms existing beliefs or preferences. Algorithmic recommendations often reinforce prior choices, creating echo chambers that intensify emotional investment and reduce exposure to alternatives. For example, a subscriber to a fitness app may be continuously presented with workouts and content aligned with their past activity, deepening engagement but limiting critical evaluation of whether the subscription still meets evolving needs. This cycle of reinforcement cultivates dependency, making cancellation psychologically challenging because it implies not just loss of service but a break from a familiar, personalised world.

Real-world cases highlight these dynamics vividly. Consider Emily, who subscribed to a premium streaming platform offering personalised film and documentary recommendations. Over time, the service's algorithm honed in on her preferences, delivering a curated selection that felt intimately attuned. This experience fostered emotional attachment; Emily felt understood and valued, justifying her monthly fee even as she found herself watching less content. The personalization mirage masked the diminishing returns, sustaining a subscription that offered comfort through tailored experience rather than substantive value. Emily's story is emblematic of broader patterns where emotional resonance supplants rational appraisal.

The tension between perceived and actual value in personalization also challenges traditional economic models of utility, which assume that consumers make decisions based on clear cost-benefit analyses. Instead, behavioural economics shows that emotional factors and perceived identity alignment heavily influence spending, especially in subscription contexts. Personalization exploits these psychological levers, converting subscribers into loyal users less through tangible benefits and more through the symbolic meaning and emotional satisfaction derived from the customised experience. This dynamic complicates efforts to foster conscious consumption and financial autonomy.

Moreover, the personalization mirage raises important ethical questions about transparency and consent. Users often lack full awareness of the data collection and algorithmic processes shaping their experiences. The opacity of recommendation systems means consumers cannot easily discern why certain content is suggested or how their behaviour influences ongoing spend. This informational asymmetry undermines informed choice, enabling platforms to manipulate engagement subtly and persistently. The ethical imperative is clear: greater transparency and user control over personalisation algorithms are essential to safeguarding autonomy and preventing exploitation.

Regulatory initiatives and emerging industry standards are beginning to address these concerns. Proposals for algorithmic accountability, data privacy protections, and clearer disclosures aim to rebalance power between consumers and platforms. Nonetheless, much responsibility rests with consumers to cultivate critical awareness of the personalization mirage. Developing digital literacy that questions algorithmic narratives and evaluates subscriptions based on explicit criteria can mitigate emotional dependency. Practical strategies include periodically reassessing subscription value detached from algorithmic influence and seeking diverse sources to counter confirmation bias.

The personalization mirage also intersects with broader cultural shifts in how value is understood and experienced. In a world saturated with choice and data, bespoke experiences promise a reprieve from overwhelm by simplifying and directing attention. Yet this simplification often comes at the cost of critical reflection and financial prudence. Recognising personalization as a commercial construct—not an unalloyed enhancement of user experience—is key to reclaiming agency. It invites a more nuanced engagement with digital services, balancing appreciation for convenience and relevance with scepticism toward engineered emotional ties.

In this light, the personalization mirage is both a marvel of technological innovation and a challenge to consumer sovereignty. It exemplifies how digital capitalism leverages psychology and data to transform spending into an ongoing emotional commitment, often detached from actual value. Understanding this dynamic equips readers to navigate the subscription economy with discernment—embracing technology's benefits while resisting the seductive illusions that perpetuate unnecessary expenditure. This critical perspective is vital for fostering a financial culture grounded in clarity, intentionality, and genuine value alignment.

Chapter 3
Financial Amnesia and Emotional Spending

Money, at its heart, is less a pile of coins or digits on a screen than a story we weave—about worth, exchange, even about who we believe ourselves to be. Yet in our digital age that story is increasingly fractured, dulled by what might aptly be called financial amnesia. The familiar cues of spending—notes passed across a counter, the weight of a signed cheque, the pause as cash leaves our hands—have largely vanished. With them goes the emotional anchor that once made our financial lives tangible. What was once a mindful practice of budgeting risks devolving into a blur of automatic transactions, detached from the memory and meaning that lend money its sense of gravity. This chapter traces that dislocation: how digital payments erode the emotional register of our spending and, in turn, set the stage for deeper, more insidious habits of emotional expenditure.

To understand financial amnesia, one must first recognise its kinship with memory itself. Just as the mind encodes and recalls moments to form a coherent sense of self, so too do we need to register our exchanges with money to sustain a conscious relationship with it. But digital payments, almost by design, interrupt this process. Subscriptions renew in silence, apps remember our card numbers, and purchases occur with a mere tap or whispered command. These frictionless flows strip away the small frictions that once forced us to notice, to feel. The emotional trace fades, transactions lose their salience, and the feedback loops that anchor spending in awareness disintegrate. What remains is a softened vigilance, a susceptibility to drift through one's financial terrain half-asleep, guided more by habit than by choice.

Layered upon this forgetting is something subtler: what could be called the dopamine budget. Subscription services—particularly in the realms of entertainment, food delivery, and gaming—trade not in simple goods but in neurochemically primed experiences. They borrow freely from the playbook of addiction science, employing intermittent rewards, bright sensory cues, and social validation to keep us hooked. Each engagement lights up the brain's reward circuitry, releasing dopamine, the chemical marker of pleasure and anticipation. The result is not rational calculation but conditioning: a pull to return, to repeat, to pay again. In this way, money flows less according to utility and more as tribute to an emotional loop engineered by design.

Here we meet what psychologists term emotional subscription dependencies. Loneliness, boredom, anxiety, the nagging edge of insecurity—emotions intensified by the pace and isolation of contemporary life—push people into sustained relationships with digital services. These platforms soothe or distract, becoming surrogate companions or coping mechanisms. The monthly fee ceases to represent objective value; it becomes the price of solace, of continuity, of reassurance. That spending, masked as convenience or harmless indulgence, is often left unexamined, normalised into the background hum of everyday consumption. Part of this chapter's work is to hold up a mirror, to encourage readers to trace the contours of their own emotional money patterns and, in so doing, reclaim a measure of agency.

Complicating matters still further is the illusion of endless choice. Digital platforms celebrate their abundance, inviting us into seemingly limitless libraries of content or products. Yet the psychology of choice tells another story: too many options can stifle rather than liberate. Decision fatigue sets in, satisfaction diminishes, and engagement becomes shallow. The streaming service, with its boundless catalogue and algorithmic nudges, epitomises this paradox. Instead of empowerment, one finds paralysis; instead of fulfilment, a restless dissatisfaction. The more there is on offer, the less meaningful any of it feels. And so we browse, dabble, and pay—caught in a cycle that drains not just money but also attention and energy. This excess of choice, rather than strengthening autonomy, feeds financial amnesia, fragmenting focus and muting intentionality.

In charting these forces, the discussion draws on diverse fields—neuroscience, behavioural economics, addiction research, psychology—braiding together their insights to create a textured portrait of how culture, cognition, and technology conspire to reshape spending. Real-world examples serve as touchstones, ensuring the ideas remain grounded in lived experience rather than drifting into abstraction. The aim is not only to expose the mechanisms at work but to furnish readers with practices of awareness—ways of noticing, questioning, and resisting.

As you move through this chapter, consider it an invitation. Not a reprimand, but a call to examine your financial life with fresh eyes. To see money not simply as figures in a ledger but as threads woven into your emotional and cognitive fabric. Financial amnesia, after all, is not a personal flaw; it is a systemic condition, fostered by technologies and cultures designed to obscure. To recognise it is to take the first step towards countering it—towards transforming budgeting from a passive sequence into a deliberate act of alignment, one that restores both clarity and control amid the swirl of digital ease and emotional entanglement.

Money Without Memory

The relationship between money and memory is far more intimate and complex than it may initially appear. At its essence, personal budgeting is not merely a matter of arithmetic or record-keeping; it is a cognitive process deeply intertwined with how our brains encode, retain, and recall financial experiences. Yet, the modern landscape of digital payments—characterised by seamless transactions, automatic renewals, and minimal physical interaction—has profoundly disrupted this relationship. This disruption creates what might be termed *money without memory*: a state in which expenditures occur without leaving a durable emotional or cognitive imprint, undermining the very foundations of conscious financial management.

To appreciate this phenomenon, it is instructive to consider the neuroscience of memory formation. Human memory operates through stages of encoding, consolidation, and retrieval, processes that are influenced by attention, emotional salience, and contextual cues. Spending money is not simply a mechanical exchange but an experience that ideally engages these cognitive systems, embedding financial decisions within the broader narrative of one's life and priorities. Traditionally, tangible transactions—handing over cash, signing receipts—provide sensory and emotional stimuli that enhance encoding. These cues create a vivid trace, enabling recall and reflection that inform future budgeting choices. This cognitive anchoring connects spending with values, intentions, and consequences, fostering financial self-awareness.

Digital payments, however, radically attenuate these sensory and emotional markers. Contactless card taps, stored payment credentials, and automated billing remove physical and psychological friction from transactions. While this facilitates convenience and efficiency, it also blunts the experiential quality of spending. Without the conscious act of approval, the brain is less likely to engage in deep encoding, resulting in shallow memory traces. This *attenuation of emotional registration* weakens the cognitive feedback loop that budgets rely upon, transforming financial outflows into abstract, background processes rather than meaningful events. In effect, money is spent without being *felt*, creating a dissonance between action and awareness.

Empirical research underscores this cognitive gap. Studies comparing payment modalities find that consumers pay more when using credit cards or digital wallets compared to cash, largely because the physical pain of parting with tangible currency is diminished. Neuroscientific evidence reveals decreased activation in brain regions associated with loss and pain during digital transactions. This diminished neural response correlates with reduced spending inhibition and weaker memory of purchases. Thus, the form of payment significantly shapes not only spending behaviour but also the mental representations that underlie financial control.

Real-world examples demonstrate how money without memory manifests in everyday life. Consider the rise of subscription services and microtransactions, where recurring charges silently siphon funds without discrete decision points. Many consumers report surprise or disbelief upon reviewing bank statements, unable to recall the full range of automatic payments debited each month. This disconnect reflects a failure of emotional registration; the brain's diminished encoding of these low-friction payments creates blind spots that impair budgeting accuracy. The invisibility of these transactions extends beyond mere forgetfulness—it is a structural consequence of the payment environment itself.

This phenomenon has profound implications for personal financial health. Budgeting is fundamentally a practice of reflection—an iterative process of comparing intentions with outcomes, adjusting behaviour based on past experience. When memory traces of spending are attenuated, this reflective process is compromised. Consumers lose the ability to intuitively monitor cash flow, anticipate shortfalls, or evaluate the value derived from expenditures. The resulting *financial amnesia* fosters overspending, reduces saving capacity, and erodes confidence in financial decision-making. Moreover, it diminishes the emotional connection to money as a finite resource, shifting consumption into an automated, unexamined domain.

The distortion introduced by digital payments also intersects with broader cultural and technological trends. The ubiquity of smartphones, digital wallets, and one-click purchasing creates an ecosystem optimised for ease rather than engagement. While these innovations democratise access and streamline commerce, they simultaneously disembed spending from the embodied and cognitive experiences that sustain mindful budgeting. This trade-off challenges conventional assumptions that greater convenience unequivocally enhances consumer welfare. Instead, it reveals a tension between efficiency and awareness—a tension that demands deliberate management.

Addressing money without memory requires both cognitive and practical interventions. At the cognitive level, cultivating *mindful spending* practices encourages active engagement with financial transactions, reinserting intentionality and emotional salience into the process. Techniques such as conscious pausing before purchase, journaling financial decisions, or associating expenses with personal values help reinforce memory encoding. Practically, tools that aggregate and visualise expenditures—such as budgeting apps that categorise transactions and provide alerts—can supplement diminished memory, externalising cognitive load and fostering insight.

Yet, these individual strategies must be understood within systemic contexts. Financial institutions, payment platforms, and subscription services wield considerable influence over how money is experienced. Ethical design principles that prioritise transparency, user control, and meaningful interaction can counteract the cognitive flattening induced by frictionless payments. Features such as detailed receipts, timely reminders, and simplified cancellation processes restore moments of reflection and decision, bridging the gap between transaction and memory. Regulatory frameworks that mandate such standards further support consumer empowerment.

This interplay between memory and money also invites philosophical reflection on the nature of financial agency. Budgeting, when viewed as a narrative construction grounded in memory, becomes an act of self-authorship. It affirms autonomy by linking present choices to past experiences and future aspirations. The erosion of this narrative through digital disembedding threatens not only financial outcomes but the coherence of selfhood itself. Reclaiming memory in money management is thus integral to preserving the integrity of personal agency amid technological transformation.

Ultimately, *money without memory* challenges readers to reconsider the invisible dynamics shaping their financial lives. It calls for a heightened awareness of how payment modalities influence cognition and emotion, urging a proactive stance that reengages the mind's natural faculties in budgeting. Through understanding and addressing this distortion, individuals can restore the reflective capacity essential for financial clarity and control. This chapter serves as a foundation for such renewal, illuminating the path from automated abstraction back to mindful, memory-infused money management.

The Dopamine Budget

Subscription services in entertainment, food delivery, and gaming industries have become masters at tapping into a fundamental human mechanism: the brain's reward circuitry. This mechanism, centred around the neurotransmitter dopamine, governs motivation, pleasure, and learning, shaping behaviours from the mundane to the addictive. The concept of a *dopamine budget* encapsulates how these services strategically engage our neural reward systems to encourage sustained use—and by extension, ongoing financial commitment.

Understanding this neurobiological entanglement is critical to recognising why subscription spending often transcends rational choice, evolving into a cycle fuelled by craving and emotional gratification rather than conscious evaluation.

Dopamine's role in reward processing is nuanced yet pivotal. Contrary to common misconception, dopamine does not simply signal pleasure but rather encodes the anticipation and motivation to seek rewards. This anticipatory function drives goal-directed behaviours, reinforcing actions that predict positive outcomes. Subscription platforms exploit this by delivering variable and intermittent rewards—new content, surprise offers, gamified achievements—that continuously stimulate dopamine release. This unpredictable reinforcement schedule, similar to that found in gambling or addictive behaviours, creates a potent motivational pull. Users experience a neurological "high" not just from consumption but from the anticipation and uncertainty surrounding each new engagement.

Consider streaming platforms like Netflix or Spotify, which employ algorithms to curate personalised content libraries that update regularly. The promise of discovering a new favourite show or song taps directly into the dopamine system's sensitivity to novelty and reward prediction errors—instances where outcomes exceed expectations. Each new release or recommendation becomes a mini dopamine trigger, compelling users to return repeatedly. While this enhances user experience, it also cultivates habitual consumption patterns that can be difficult to disengage from, particularly as the subscription model incentivises continuous payment regardless of actual usage.

Food delivery apps extend this dynamic into the realm of immediate gratification. The simple act of ordering a meal, facilitated by seamless interfaces and real-time tracking, creates a cascade of anticipatory dopamine spikes—from browsing menus to receiving delivery notifications. The sensory pleasure of food combined with the psychological reward of convenience amplifies engagement. Importantly, these platforms often employ push notifications and personalised promotions timed to exploit moments of vulnerability or boredom, further driving impulsive spending. This neurobehavioural loop elevates spending beyond nutritional needs into an arena of emotional reward.

Gaming subscriptions provide perhaps the clearest illustration of dopamine budget mechanics in action. Free-to-play models supplemented by subscription tiers or microtransactions are meticulously engineered to sustain engagement through reward schedules, social competition, and achievement systems. Players experience dopamine bursts when unlocking new levels, earning badges, or receiving social recognition—reinforcements that maintain motivation and justify ongoing financial outlays. Addiction science identifies these patterns as analogous to substance dependency, with similar neural circuits implicated. The line between leisure and compulsive engagement blurs, raising important considerations about consumer vulnerability and ethical design.

This neurobiological exploitation challenges classical economic assumptions of rational consumer behaviour. The dopamine budget reveals how spending decisions are often unconsciously driven by reward-seeking circuits rather than deliberate calculation. Emotional gratification and habit formation can overshadow cost-benefit analyses, leading to sustained subscriptions even when practical value diminishes. This insight reframes budgeting as a psychological as well as financial endeavour, necessitating strategies that acknowledge and address underlying neural drivers.

Recognising the dopamine budget also invites ethical reflection on the responsibilities of service providers. While engagement is a legitimate business goal, designing systems that hijack reward pathways to foster dependence crosses into ethically ambiguous territory. Transparency about behavioural strategies, offering meaningful user controls, and supporting healthy usage patterns are essential to respecting consumer autonomy. Regulatory frameworks increasingly scrutinise these practices, reflecting societal concerns about digital addiction and financial exploitation.

For consumers, awareness of the dopamine budget can empower more mindful engagement. Developing skills to recognise reward-driven impulses, pausing before renewal decisions, and setting explicit spending limits can mitigate compulsive tendencies.

Incorporating reflective practices—such as journaling emotional triggers linked to subscription use or seeking alternative fulfilment sources—helps disentangle spending from neurochemical conditioning. Technology tools that monitor usage patterns and alert users to changes in engagement can serve as external supports, bridging cognitive gaps induced by dopamine-driven behaviours.

The dopamine budget exemplifies the intricate interplay between brain chemistry, technology design, and financial behaviour in the subscription economy. It underscores that spending is not merely a rational transaction but a complex psychological act influenced by powerful neurobiological forces. By illuminating these dynamics, readers gain crucial insight into the hidden drivers of subscription spending, equipping them to reclaim agency and cultivate budgeting practices grounded in awareness rather than compulsion. This understanding is vital for navigating modern financial landscapes where pleasure, addiction, and economic decision-making intersect with unprecedented complexity.

Emotional Subscription Dependencies

In a world increasingly mediated by digital connections and instant gratification, subscriptions have evolved from mere services into emotional crutches that many lean on to soothe deeper psychological needs. The phenomenon of *emotional subscription dependencies* reflects how loneliness, boredom, and insecurity—conditions that are both widespread and intensifying—fuel continued engagement with subscription services beyond their utilitarian value. These dependencies are not incidental side effects but intrinsic to how subscription models are designed and experienced. Understanding this dynamic requires a close examination of the emotional landscapes that underlie spending, revealing why certain subscriptions persist as sources of comfort, distraction, or identity reinforcement even when they no longer serve practical purposes.

Loneliness, often described as an epidemic of modern life, creates fertile ground for emotional spending. Humans are inherently social creatures, wired for connection and belonging. When social bonds weaken or become insufficient, individuals naturally seek substitutes to fill the void. Subscription services, particularly those offering entertainment, social interaction, or curated content, provide an accessible and immediate form of companionship. Platforms like Netflix, social media apps, or online learning communities extend an invitation to engage, distract, and occupy time—functions that can momentarily assuage feelings of isolation. However, this palliative effect can subtly morph into dependency as the service becomes a habitual go-to for emotional regulation, blurring the line between choice and compulsion. The financial cost, often dispersed and automatic, slips beneath the threshold of conscious evaluation, entrenching the subscription in daily routines and emotional cycles.

Boredom, a state characterised by restlessness and dissatisfaction, similarly propels ongoing subscription use. In contemporary societies where constant stimulation is readily available, boredom paradoxically intensifies, prompting individuals to seek novel experiences or distractions. Subscription services cater to this demand by offering endless streams of content, gamified challenges, or on-demand goods. The relentless availability creates a feedback loop: boredom triggers engagement, engagement provides temporary relief, but over time the threshold for satisfaction rises, requiring ever more frequent or intense interaction. This escalation fosters spending patterns driven less by need and more by the avoidance of discomfort. The psychological interplay between boredom and subscription consumption challenges simplistic notions of rational budgeting, highlighting how emotional states shape financial behaviour.

Insecurity, whether financial, social, or existential, also contributes to emotional subscription dependencies. Subscriptions can function as symbolic investments in self-improvement, status, or control, promising growth or belonging in uncertain contexts. Educational platforms, fitness apps, and wellness services often market themselves as pathways to better versions of oneself, appealing to anxieties about adequacy or success. This aspirational messaging resonates emotionally, encouraging sustained financial commitment even when actual engagement wanes. The tension between desired identity and lived reality creates cognitive dissonance, where cancelling a subscription feels like relinquishing hope or admitting failure. Consequently, insecurity anchors subscriptions as emotional lifelines, complicating decisions about value and cost.

Recognising these emotional drivers is essential for cultivating financial and psychological autonomy. The chapter offers guided prompts designed to help readers identify their own *emotional money patterns*, a process that combines introspection with practical budgeting. Questions such as: "When do I feel compelled to engage with or renew a subscription?" "What emotions am I trying to soothe or avoid through this spending?" and "How does this subscription relate to my sense of self or social connection?" encourage nuanced self-exploration. This reflective practice reveals patterns that often operate beneath conscious awareness, illuminating the emotional logic that sustains spending and opening pathways for intentional change.

Critically, emotional subscription dependencies challenge conventional economic models predicated on rational choice and utility maximisation. They underscore the intertwined nature of emotion and finance, where money becomes a medium for managing psychological states rather than merely acquiring goods or services. This insight calls for integrating emotional literacy into financial education and budgeting practices, recognising that effective money management must address not only numbers but also feelings and motivations.

Moreover, the phenomenon invites ethical reflection on the role of subscription providers. While offering value and convenience, these services also exploit human vulnerabilities—loneliness, boredom, insecurity—to foster engagement and revenue. The design of platforms that leverage social validation, continuous novelty, and aspirational narratives raises questions about corporate responsibility and consumer protection. Transparent communication, user empowerment, and ethical design principles are crucial to mitigating the risks of emotional dependency.

Balancing the benefits and risks of subscription services requires cultivating resilience and self-awareness. Developing alternative strategies for emotional regulation—such as building real-world social connections, engaging in purposeful activities, and practising mindfulness—can reduce reliance on subscriptions as emotional crutches. Financially, integrating emotional awareness into budgeting promotes decisions aligned with both practical needs and psychological well-being.

Emotional subscription dependencies reveal a deeply human dimension of modern financial life, where money, mind, and emotion converge in complex patterns. By exploring the roots of these dependencies and providing tools for reflection and change, this chapter equips readers to navigate the subscription economy with greater clarity, compassion, and control. It opens a vital dialogue about how we spend—not only with our wallets but with our hearts—and how reclaiming that dialogue can transform both financial health and emotional resilience.

The Lie of Infinite Choice

The promise of *infinite choice*—an endless buffet of content, products, and services available at the tap of a screen—is often heralded as a hallmark of modern consumer empowerment. Streaming platforms, online marketplaces, and digital subscriptions trumpet this abundance as a gateway to freedom, diversity, and personalised satisfaction. Yet, beneath this glossy veneer lies a paradox: rather than liberating consumers, the overwhelming volume of options frequently breeds confusion, frustration, and dissatisfaction. The abundance that was supposed to empower instead induces a phenomenon known as *choice fatigue*, a cognitive overload that undermines decision-making and can erode both enjoyment and financial wellbeing.

Psychological research over decades has documented the limits of human decision-making in the face of abundant options. While a small array of choices facilitates comparison and preference expression, exponentially increasing alternatives strain cognitive resources. The brain's capacity for effective evaluation diminishes as options multiply, leading to longer deliberation times, increased anxiety, and often, poorer choices. This *paradox of choice*, popularised by psychologist Barry Schwartz, explains why more options do not always translate into greater satisfaction—in fact, the opposite often occurs. Consumers can become overwhelmed, defaulting to indecision or impulsive shortcuts, both of which undermine intentional budgeting and mindful consumption.

Streaming platforms epitomise this paradox. Netflix, Amazon Prime Video, Disney+, and countless niche services collectively offer libraries containing tens of thousands of titles. The sheer scale promises something for everyone, yet many users report difficulty choosing what to watch, spending more time browsing than viewing. This experience is not trivial; it shapes user engagement, satisfaction, and ultimately subscription value perception. Studies reveal that excessive choice correlates with reduced enjoyment and increased regret post-decision, phenomena linked to cognitive exhaustion and the expectation of a "better" option remaining unseen. For subscribers, this can mean ongoing payments for services they rarely use fully or that fail to meet emotional needs, trapped by the inertia of choice overload.

Beyond streaming, the illusion of infinite choice extends to other subscription-based sectors such as music, fitness, and meal delivery. Users faced with myriad playlists, workout programmes, or meal plans experience similar paralysis. The cognitive burden of selecting from diverse offerings can diminish perceived control, ironically eroding the very autonomy these services promise. The resulting dissatisfaction may lead to subscription churn, multiple overlapping services, or defaulting to the cheapest option without regard to quality—behaviours that complicate budgeting and obscure true value.

This tension between choice abundance and consumer experience raises important conceptual questions about value and agency. Does more choice reflect genuine empowerment, or is it a commodification strategy that leverages cognitive vulnerabilities? Many platforms employ recommendation algorithms intended to personalise and narrow options, yet these tools can inadvertently reinforce choice fatigue by presenting vast quantities of seemingly tailored but ultimately overwhelming content. Moreover, the illusion of control provided by choice can mask manipulative design practices that prioritise engagement metrics over user wellbeing, deepening dependency without delivering proportional satisfaction.

Ethically, the proliferation of choice invites scrutiny of business models that commodify consumer attention and decision-making capacity. The pressure to maintain subscriptions, despite dissatisfaction or underuse, reflects a structural imbalance where consumers face cognitive and emotional costs not fully disclosed or compensated. Regulators and consumer advocates increasingly call for transparency, simplified offerings, and user-centric design that honours the cognitive limits of decision-makers rather than exploiting them.

Practical strategies to navigate the lie of infinite choice begin with cultivating *choice architecture*—the deliberate design of environments that facilitate better decisions. Consumers can benefit from imposing self-constraints, such as limiting the number of active subscriptions, setting clear usage goals, or adopting minimalist principles in consumption. Reflective budgeting practices that focus on value rather than volume help counteract the impulse to accumulate options unnecessarily. Tools that aggregate subscription data and usage metrics provide empirical clarity, helping users prioritise and prune choices aligned with personal values.

The cultural dimension of this paradox merits attention. The narrative of abundance as progress shapes societal expectations, making dissatisfaction with choice feel like personal failure rather than systemic design outcome. Challenging this narrative involves reframing satisfaction and success in terms of *meaningful engagement* rather than quantity. Embracing limits and intentionality in consumption restores agency and aligns spending with deeper goals, transforming budgeting into a practice of thoughtful curation rather than overwhelmed acquiescence.

In exploring the lie of infinite choice, this chapter invites readers to confront the cognitive and emotional complexities underpinning modern consumption. It reveals that empowerment lies not in the unrestrained expansion of options but in the conscious management of attention, intention, and value. Understanding this dynamic equips readers to reclaim clarity and control amid the noise, fostering financial and psychological wellbeing in a world awash with possibilities yet starved of meaningful direction.

Chapter 4
Budgeting as Narrative Therapy

Every bank statement, though often skimmed for figures alone, is far more than a tidy ledger of debits and credits. It is, in truth, a kind of diary—layered with values, anxieties, unspoken hopes, and ingrained habits. Read in this way, budgeting ceases to be a dry exercise in arithmetic; it becomes a practice of self-exploration, a means of shaping meaning from money. This chapter proposes precisely that reframing: to treat budgeting as a form of narrative therapy, an opportunity to author a financial life that reflects genuine priorities rather than unconscious repetition. Such a shift is neither simple nor cosmetic. It calls into question long-standing habits of reactive spending, the silences we keep around money, and the avoidance that so often masks discomfort. What emerges instead is a conscious dialogue—with one's finances, one's emotions, and ultimately one's sense of identity.

Look closely at a statement and you will find the story it tells is both intricate and revealing. Each outflow, each line item, carries the trace of a choice: some mark celebration, the quiet reward for effort; others are camouflage for anxiety, or stand-in companions for solitude; still others reveal the tug of routine, the comfort of the familiar. By listening to these unspoken tales rather than dismissing them as mere transactions, one begins to glimpse the emotional undercurrents of financial behaviour. A journaling exercise introduced in this chapter animates this idea: *If this expense could speak, what would it say?* It is a deceptively simple prompt, yet it opens a door to deeper reflection, coaxing us to hear what money, in its silent way, has been trying to tell us. Here, budgeting becomes less a table of numbers than a dialogue between past choices and future intentions, a process in which clarity and agency can finally take root.

The book argues for a decisive pivot—from default to design. Instead of treating the budget as a weary catalogue of obligations, it can be approached as a creative blueprint for a life aligned with authentic values. The difference is profound. Rather than acquiescing to patterns inherited or unconsciously repeated, individuals become active sculptors of their financial landscape.

Consider the story, retold here, of a family who succeeded in halving their household expenses without falling into deprivation. They achieved this balance not through self-denial, but by lifting up purchases that held meaning and trimming away what did not. Their example reminds us that discipline, when born of intentionality, can enable flourishing rather than constrict it.

But no genuine narrative therapy can avoid the shadows—those regions where money intersects with shame and silence. Many find financial secrecy or emotional repression quietly eroding both wellbeing and solvency. The sense of guilt over spending, or the stigma of financial difficulty, has a way of breeding avoidance, making honest reckoning all but impossible. This chapter addresses that silence head-on. Through guided prompts and structured reflections, readers are encouraged to name their fears, to acknowledge vulnerabilities, and in doing so, to unfasten the stigma that clings so stubbornly to money. Such openness not only aids psychological healing but also yields practical rewards: accountability sharpens, decisions grow clearer, and the path forward feels less fraught.

Another recurring pattern deserves attention: the insidious *"I deserve this"* loop. Reward spending, particularly in the age of one-click subscriptions, often masquerades as self-care but can become a cycle of emotional compensation. Here, money is used to soothe stress, to assert control, or to reinforce an identity under strain. Yet these gestures, however comforting in the moment, rarely nourish for long. The chapter offers tools to untangle this knot—strategies to discern genuine sustenance from fleeting gratification, to recognise the subtle triggers that spark impulsive outlay, and to step out of the cycle with greater self-awareness.

Drawing on insights from psychology, behavioural economics, and financial therapy, this approach lays down a robust framework for viewing budgeting as narrative work. Theory, however, is never left untethered; real-world stories and practical exercises ground the discussion, guiding readers in translating ideas into lived practice. Above all, the model respects the complexity of human motivation. It does not reduce money to sterile calculation, but recognises it as entangled with emotion, identity, and meaning.

To embrace budgeting as narrative therapy is to reclaim authorship of one's financial story. It is to exchange a narrative of scarcity and obligation for one of abundance, alignment, and purpose. This reframing asks readers to approach money not as passive consumers within the machinery of the subscription economy, but as deliberate creators of their financial futures. What results is not merely improved balance sheets, but a richer relationship with money itself—marked by curiosity, compassion, and a conscious hand on the pen that writes the ongoing story.

The Story Your Bank Statement Tells

The pages of a bank statement are often treated as mere numerical records—lines of data listing transactions that cumulatively reflect the flow of money in and out of an account. Yet beneath these figures lies a richer, untapped narrative: a story about who we are, what we value, what we fear, and how we habitually live. To engage with a bank statement merely as a financial ledger is to miss the profound psychological and emotional textures embedded in each expense. This subchapter invites readers to reimagine their monthly expenses not as cold numbers but as vibrant chapters in a personal financial story—one that reveals motivations, conflicts, and patterns ripe for exploration and transformation.

When viewed as a narrative, each expense becomes a character with a voice, intentions, and emotional resonance. A subscription fee may speak of comfort or avoidance; a coffee purchase may whisper of routine or social connection; a missed payment might murmur of anxiety or neglect. By personifying expenses, we shift from detached calculation to engaged reflection. This narrative lens illuminates how financial behaviours are often proxies for deeper psychological states—hope, shame, desire, or fear—and how money choices interlace with identity and habit. In doing so, budgeting transforms from a mechanical task into a form of storytelling and self-discovery.

Central to this reframing is a simple but powerful journaling exercise: *"If this expense could talk, what would it say?"* This prompt encourages readers to pause and give voice to their spending, inviting imagination and emotional insight. For example, a gym membership might confess, "I represent your aspirations for health and discipline, but you rarely visit me," while an online shopping charge might admit, "I fill your boredom and ease your stress, even as I burden your budget." Through such personification, readers confront the mixed messages their money sends, enabling them to recognise contradictions, ambivalences, and unspoken needs embedded in their financial life.

This narrative approach also reveals patterns that traditional budgeting often overlooks. Recurring charges may form a subplot of complacency or inertia; impulsive buys might be episodic plot twists driven by emotional triggers. Recognising these threads allows individuals to intervene deliberately, rewriting their financial stories with intention rather than habit. The exercise fosters a shift from passive receipt of expenses to active authorship—empowering readers to interrogate why they spend as they do, what they are trying to communicate to themselves through their money, and how they might realign spending with authentic values.

Case studies exemplify this transformation. Take Hannah, who upon journaling her bank statement realised that many small streaming subscriptions symbolised her desire for social connection during isolation. Though rationally expendable, these expenses carried emotional weight, serving as digital companionship. By acknowledging this, she consciously chose to consolidate her subscriptions and invest saved funds into occasional in-person gatherings, reshaping her financial narrative to better reflect her evolving needs. Such examples underscore how the story your bank statement tells is dynamic and capable of being retold to foster wellbeing and clarity.

This narrative perspective challenges conventional budgeting paradigms that prioritise austerity, discipline, or external metrics of success. Instead, it situates budgeting within the lived experience of selfhood, emotion, and meaning. It demands that we honour the complexity of financial choices as expressions of our inner worlds, not just economic transactions. This shift has practical implications: budgeting becomes less about rigid restrictions and more about compassionate inquiry and creative problem-solving.

Engaging with expenses as narrators also opens pathways to confront financial fears and shame. Money is often a taboo subject, cloaked in silence and secrecy, which impedes honest reflection and growth. Giving voice to expenses disrupts this silence, fostering dialogue between conscious and unconscious aspects of financial life. It invites empathy towards oneself, recognising that money habits are shaped by context, history, and emotional needs rather than mere rationality. This compassionate stance softens resistance and opens space for meaningful change.

The narrative framing further enriches financial literacy by integrating psychological insight with practical action. Readers learn to decode the symbolic language of spending, fostering a deeper relationship with money that supports sustainable habits. The exercise encourages regular reflection, turning budgeting into an ongoing conversation rather than a one-off chore. It empowers readers to approach money with curiosity and nuance, cultivating financial mindfulness that is both intellectually rigorous and emotionally intelligent.

Ultimately, the story your bank statement tells is a profound resource for self-knowledge and transformation. By listening attentively to the voices within your expenses, you reclaim authorship over your financial life. This narrative engagement disrupts automatic patterns, reveals hidden motives, and aligns spending with authentic values. It invites you to write a financial story that honours not only your economic realities but your emotional truths, creating a foundation for budgeting that is as much about meaning as it is about money.

From Default to Design

Many individuals navigate their finances in a reactive mode—responding to bills, subscriptions, and obligations as they arise, often feeling trapped in an unrelenting cycle of payments that seem both necessary and burdensome. This *default* mode of financial management rarely invites reflection or intentionality; it reduces budgeting to a passive exercise in compliance rather than a proactive process of designing a life aligned with one's values and aspirations. Shifting from default to design is not simply a matter of budgeting tactics but a profound mindset transformation that empowers individuals and families to reclaim agency over their money and, by extension, their lives.

This shift entails moving beyond the rote fulfilment of financial obligations to an intentional crafting of spending patterns that reflect conscious choices rather than inherited habits or societal pressures. When spending becomes an act of design, each expense is scrutinised for its alignment with personal priorities, enabling a dynamic interplay between resource allocation and life goals. This reframing dissolves the dichotomy between discipline and deprivation, revealing budgeting as a creative practice that can enhance wellbeing and fulfilment. It invites a reassessment of what constitutes "necessary" expenses, emphasising value and meaning over default acceptance.

The transformative potential of this approach is vividly illustrated by the experience of the Thompsons, a middle-income family of four who managed to halve their monthly expenses without feeling deprived. Faced with mounting debt and stress, the Thompsons embarked on a radical redesign of their financial life. They began by mapping their spending against their core values—prioritising health, education, and quality time over material accumulation and convenience. This process revealed numerous habitual expenses—multiple streaming subscriptions, frequent dining out, and redundant insurance policies—that neither served their values nor enhanced their quality of life.

Instead of cutting indiscriminately, the Thompsons applied a principle of *value-based pruning*: they cancelled or consolidated subscriptions that delivered little joy or utility, embraced home-cooked meals as family rituals rather than chores, and renegotiated essential services to better fit their usage patterns. Importantly, they reframed budgeting as a collective family project, fostering open dialogue and shared commitment. This collective ownership transformed budgeting from an isolated chore into a source of connection and empowerment. As a result, their financial redesign not only improved their economic situation but also strengthened family cohesion and reduced stress, demonstrating that deliberate design can yield holistic benefits beyond mere cost-cutting.

This case highlights several critical insights. First, budgeting as design requires a clear articulation of values and priorities, which serve as the compass guiding financial decisions. Values function as filters, enabling discernment between expenses that nourish and those that drain. Second, intentional budgeting demands ongoing evaluation and flexibility, recognising that life circumstances and aspirations evolve. Third, the emotional dimension of money management is central: addressing fears, habits, and attachments with compassion facilitates sustainable change. Finally, collaboration and communication—whether within families or support networks—are powerful accelerators of successful financial redesign.

Shifting from default to design also involves confronting societal narratives that equate consumption with success and happiness. The prevailing cultural scripts often encourage passive spending patterns driven by marketing, peer pressure, or status anxiety. Breaking free from these scripts requires critical reflection and courage, especially as it may involve redefining identity and social belonging in less materialistic terms. This reorientation fosters resilience against consumerist pressures and supports financial choices rooted in authenticity.

Practically, embracing budgeting as design invites the integration of tools and methods that promote visibility, intentionality, and creativity. Techniques such as zero-based budgeting, financial mood boards, and value inventories help externalise and clarify intentions. Digital tools that visualise spending patterns support reflective engagement and empower informed adjustments. Importantly, design thinking—emphasising iteration, experimentation, and user-centric perspectives—can be adapted to personal finance, enabling continuous refinement rather than one-time fixes.

This paradigm shift also challenges the framing of budgeting as sacrifice or austerity. Instead, it positions budgeting as an act of self-care and life curation, aligning resource management with wellbeing. This perspective encourages readers to envision their finances as tools for enabling desired experiences, relationships, and growth, transforming money from a source of stress into a vehicle for intentional living.

As readers engage with this chapter, they are invited to begin their own journey from default financial habits to purposeful design. Through reflection, experimentation, and commitment, budgeting becomes an empowering practice that honours both practical realities and deeper aspirations. The Thompsons' story is not an isolated anomaly but a testament to what is possible when individuals reclaim control and creativity over their financial lives, crafting stories of resilience, alignment, and flourishing amid the complexities of the subscription economy.

Money, Shame, and Silence

Money is rarely a neutral subject. It carries with it a heavy weight of emotional charge—shame, guilt, fear—that often silences open dialogue and distorts our relationship with personal finance. The triad of *money, shame, and silence* forms a cycle that traps many in secrecy and emotional repression, hindering clarity, accountability, and growth. This subchapter addresses this profound yet frequently overlooked aspect of financial life, illuminating how shame operates beneath the surface of budgeting struggles and how breaking silence with self-compassion and structured reflection can initiate healing and empowerment.

At the heart of money-related shame is the stigma attached to perceived financial inadequacy. Societal norms and cultural narratives valorise wealth, success, and consumption, implicitly equating financial difficulty or restraint with failure or moral weakness. Those who struggle with debt, budgeting, or simply navigating the complex modern economy often internalise these messages, experiencing shame that discourages honest self-appraisal or disclosure. This emotional repression creates a barrier to effective financial management: when money problems are shrouded in secrecy, they fester unaddressed, eroding mental health and perpetuating dysfunctional patterns. Silence becomes a protective yet isolating mechanism, shielding the individual from judgment but simultaneously cutting off avenues for support and learning.

Research in psychology underscores how shame related to money is both pervasive and damaging. Studies reveal that financial shame correlates strongly with anxiety, depression, and lower self-esteem, compounding the stressors that accompany economic insecurity. Unlike guilt, which focuses on specific behaviours and can motivate reparative action, shame attacks the self, engendering feelings of unworthiness and paralysis. This distinction is critical: interventions that cultivate self-compassion—an attitude of kindness and understanding toward one's struggles—can counteract shame's corrosive effects, fostering resilience and constructive engagement.

Breaking the cycle of silence requires deliberate strategies to foster open dialogue and internal acceptance. The chapter introduces structured prompts designed to guide readers through reflective conversations with themselves and trusted others. Questions such as "What feelings arise when I look at my financial situation?" or "What stories do I tell myself about my worth in relation to money?" invite exploration of underlying emotions and beliefs. These exercises serve as tools for naming and normalising shame, transforming it from an invisible burden into an acknowledged experience subject to change.

Importantly, cultivating self-compassion is central to this process. Drawing on the work of Kristin Neff and others, the chapter emphasises that self-compassion involves recognising one's shared humanity, embracing imperfections without harsh judgment, and responding to suffering with kindness. This orientation creates a safe inner space where financial challenges can be confronted with curiosity and patience rather than blame. Through self-compassionate reflection, budgeting becomes less a test of character and more a practice of care and learning.

Real-world examples highlight the transformative power of breaking financial silence. Consider Marcus, who had long concealed his mounting credit card debt from family and friends, fearing stigma and shame. When he began journaling about his money fears and eventually confided in a close friend, he experienced a profound release of emotional tension. This openness enabled him to seek practical advice, restructure his finances, and adopt a budgeting approach rooted in self-acceptance rather than punishment. Marcus's story illustrates how confronting shame and silence catalyses both emotional relief and tangible financial progress.

The chapter also critically examines the social and cultural dimensions that perpetuate money shame. It challenges prevailing narratives that equate financial success with personal worth, urging readers to question these value systems and adopt a more nuanced, compassionate view of economic diversity and human complexity. This broader perspective supports a cultural shift toward openness and mutual support around money, dismantling taboos that isolate individuals and families.

Ethical considerations emerge regarding how financial institutions, employers, and advisors engage with clients. Practices that stigmatise financial hardship or ignore emotional contexts risk reinforcing shame and silence. Conversely, approaches that integrate empathy, transparency, and psychological insight promote trust and empower clients to take meaningful control. The chapter advocates for a holistic paradigm in financial guidance—one that honours both numbers and narratives.

By tackling *money, shame, and silence*, this chapter equips readers with both the awareness and practical tools to transform their financial relationships. It invites a courageous engagement with vulnerability, fostering an inner climate where honesty and kindness create fertile ground for sustainable budgeting and wellbeing. This shift from repression to dialogue is not merely therapeutic; it is foundational to reclaiming agency in a subscription economy that often thrives on hidden dependencies and unspoken struggles.

The "I Deserve This" Loop

The phrase *"I deserve this"* often surfaces as a quiet justification for spending that strays beyond necessity—an emotional rationale that cushions financial decisions with self-reward, comfort, or even defiance. This seemingly benign declaration, however, can conceal a complex psychological cycle of reward spending and subscription rationalization, one that subtly erodes financial clarity and autonomy. The *"I Deserve This" loop* encapsulates how individuals repeatedly validate expenditures not purely on practical grounds, but as a means to soothe emotional needs, alleviate stress, or assert control in turbulent times. Untangling this loop is critical to understanding the emotional architecture of spending habits in a subscription-driven economy and offers a pathway to distinguish genuine nourishment from fleeting compensation.

At the core of this loop lies the intersection of self-worth and consumption. When life's pressures accumulate—be it work stress, social comparison, or personal setbacks—spending can function as a psychological balm. The act of purchasing, especially within subscription models promising convenience, pleasure, or status, triggers dopamine release, reinforcing behaviours that temporarily elevate mood or self-esteem. This neurochemical reward system, while adaptive in moderation, becomes a double-edged sword when habitual spending substitutes for deeper emotional processing. The phrase *"I deserve this"* transforms into a recurrent internal script that legitimises continued financial outflows, often detached from mindful assessment of value or sustainability.

Subscription services intensify this dynamic by embedding reward spending within seamless, recurring frameworks. The automatic renewal of streaming platforms, wellness apps, or curated boxes removes friction from consumption decisions, enabling sustained engagement that feels effortless yet financially consequential. Rationalisations multiply: "I've already paid this month," "It helps me relax," or "It supports my personal growth." These beliefs merge with the *"I Deserve This"* narrative, creating cognitive dissonance that obscures critical scrutiny. As subscriptions accumulate, the cumulative cost may exceed actual utility, but the emotional investment sustains the cycle, rendering cancellation psychologically fraught.

Real-world examples illuminate the loop's mechanics. Take Rachel, a professional who subscribes to multiple mindfulness apps, premium fitness platforms, and gourmet meal deliveries. She describes these expenses as self-care essentials, affirming her worth and managing her hectic lifestyle. Yet, upon closer reflection, Rachel recognises that actual usage is sporadic and that many services add complexity rather than relief. The justification—*"I deserve this"*—has become a habitual refrain, shielding her from confronting underlying stressors and budgetary imbalance. This recognition becomes a turning point, highlighting how emotional narratives can both support and undermine financial wellbeing.

Distinguishing *true nourishment* from *emotional compensation* requires deliberate reflection and tools that foster self-awareness. True nourishment aligns spending with sustained benefit and congruence with core values; emotional compensation often manifests as impulsive or habitual expenditure aimed at momentary relief. The chapter offers practical prompts to aid this discernment: assessing the frequency and impact of usage, evaluating emotional triggers preceding spending, and exploring alternative coping mechanisms that do not incur financial cost. These reflective exercises cultivate a mindful relationship with money, enabling readers to interrupt the loop with conscious choice rather than automatic rationalisation.

Psychological theories deepen this analysis. The concept of *affect regulation* explains how individuals use external means—including spending—to manage internal emotional states. While adaptive in moderation, reliance on consumption for emotional stability can precipitate patterns resembling behavioural addiction. Cognitive dissonance theory elucidates how justifications such as *"I deserve this"* resolve tensions between self-image and behaviour, maintaining expenditure despite financial strain. Recognising these mechanisms equips readers to question automatic narratives and engage in more balanced decision-making.

Ethical considerations arise in relation to how commercial entities exploit the *"I Deserve This"* loop. Marketing strategies often appeal to consumers' desire for reward and affirmation, framing subscriptions as deserved privileges rather than discretionary choices. The seductive language of empowerment and self-care can obscure commercial imperatives, complicating consumers' ability to disentangle authentic need from manufactured desire. Transparency, responsible marketing, and consumer education are vital counterweights to these dynamics.

Breaking the *"I Deserve This"* loop is a process requiring patience, self-compassion, and practical strategy. It involves acknowledging emotional needs without letting them dictate spending unchecked. Cultivating alternative forms of self-care—such as social connection, creative pursuits, or physical activity—can fulfill underlying desires without financial depletion. Budgeting framed as an act of respect for oneself, rather than restriction, supports this transition.

Importantly, reframing reward spending as an occasional, intentional indulgence rather than a default coping strategy restores balance and agency.

In illuminating the *"I Deserve This"* loop, this chapter provides a critical lens on the emotional underpinnings of subscription spending, moving beyond surface-level budgeting to address psychological complexity. It empowers readers to recognise and transform the narratives that sustain unnecessary expenditure, fostering financial practices that honour both economic reality and emotional wellbeing. This insight is essential for navigating the subscription economy with clarity, intention, and freedom from compulsion.

Chapter 5
Subscription Culture as Modern Serfdom

Subscription culture has, almost imperceptibly, redrawn the contours of our economic and social existence. What began as a clever business convenience—pay a steady monthly fee for access to films, music, or software—has metastasised into something larger, a dense ecosystem that reaches far beyond consumer choice. Beneath its polished surface lies a subtler transformation: we are no longer simply customers, but participants in a system that commodifies our very presence. This chapter considers subscription culture not as a benign innovation but as a contemporary form of serfdom, where recurring payments, relentless data extraction, and behavioural steering combine to weave new structures of dependence and enclosure.

At the centre of this shift is a troubling inversion: the question of who controls value and how it is drawn out of us. The old assumption—that in commercial exchanges the consumer is unequivocally the customer—has grown shaky. Many subscription platforms operate on a dual register, presenting the user as client while simultaneously treating them as product. It is not money alone that flows upstream, but data: patterns of attention, gestures of behaviour, fragments of personal life. These fragments are then refined into the raw material of algorithmic prediction, feeding systems designed to anticipate, and more insidiously to influence, our next move. What appears to us as convenience or personalisation is in fact a choreography of dependence, engineered to deepen engagement and ensure that departure feels unthinkable. Agency, in such a schema, is eroded by loops too opaque to contest.

This process dovetails neatly with a broader economic trajectory: the rise of the rentier order. Ownership, once the cornerstone of stability and independence, yields ground to access, which promises freedom but often delivers fragility. What began with music and films now extends across life's essentials—housing, mobility, even health and education. Instead of outright possession, we find ourselves tied into indefinite rentals, each renewal a quiet tax on autonomy. The appearance of flexibility disguises a new form of precariousness, as the promise of temporary use hardens into a permanent obligation.

The implications reach into cultural and social realms as well, culminating in what might aptly be called the eternal paywall. Knowledge, entertainment, even self-improvement—domains once imagined as public goods or relatively open fields—are now sliced into gated segments. Platforms, publishers, and institutions become gatekeepers, erecting walls around what once circulated more freely. Consumers shoulder not only the weight of escalating costs but also the fragmentation of cultural life into scattered, conditional access points. The ideal of a shared cultural commons recedes, replaced by a marketplace of perpetual tolls.

History casts its long shadow here. The chapter draws deliberate parallels between today's subscription snares and earlier systems of servitude: indenture, sharecropping, the various arrangements that bound labourers to cycles of debt. Such comparisons are not rhetorical flourish. They reveal how the seemingly neutral mechanism of recurring revenue may cloak patterns of bondage in new, digitised attire. Contracts, endlessly renewable and difficult to exit, become a form of chain—less visible, but binding all the same.

This, inevitably, forces us to reconsider notions of consent and choice. The glossy promise of convenience and endless options masks an imbalance of power, where the individual holds neither full information nor genuine leverage. Platforms design with retention, not wellbeing, in mind; engagement becomes the metric, not fulfilment. Ethical dilemmas abound: what does it mean to commodify attention itself, or to treat access to culture, education, even housing as a subscription privilege rather than a right? The chapter urges stronger transparency, sharper regulation, and, importantly, a cultivation of consumer literacy that equips people to recognise the mechanics at work.

Examples bring these abstractions down to earth. A family weighing the cost of juggling five streaming subscriptions, a student paying recurring fees for textbooks once purchased outright, a tenant locked into platform-mediated housing—these are not anomalies but ordinary lives shaped by the logic of perpetual rent. Such cases lend flesh to theory, revealing not only the risks but also the possibility of resistance: the moments where awareness can seed alternative choices.

In the end, the invitation of this chapter is a demanding one: to look closely at how subscription models, draped in the rhetoric of progress, subtly rewire both our finances and our cultural life. To approach them critically does not mean rejecting innovation wholesale, but to see clearly the structures of dependency they conceal. By mapping these contours of modern serfdom, we may yet imagine ways to recover autonomy, equity, and dignity within an economy that would prefer us always paying, always tethered, always just one renewal away from belonging.

You're Not the Custome

Subscription models have reshaped how we consume media, software, and services, promising convenience, personalization, and flexibility. Yet beneath this appealing surface lies a fundamental inversion of the traditional consumer relationship: *you are not the customer—you are the product.* This unsettling truth underscores a critical dynamic in many subscription ecosystems, where the user's data, attention, and behaviour are the primary commodities being harvested, analysed, and monetised. Understanding this shift from consumer sovereignty to commodification is essential for navigating the subscription economy with informed agency and ethical clarity.

At its core, the subscription business model depends heavily on continuous engagement. Retention—not one-time purchases—is the metric that drives platform growth and profitability. To sustain this engagement, companies invest heavily in data extraction and behavioural prediction technologies. Every interaction, from clicks and scrolling patterns to time spent on specific content, feeds algorithms that build detailed user profiles. These profiles enable platforms to anticipate needs, personalise experiences, and deliver targeted content and advertising designed to maximise user attention and spending. As platform economist Arun Sundararajan articulates, in this model *"users are not just consumers but sources of valuable data,"* making them, in effect, the product sold to advertisers and partners.

This commodification extends far beyond obvious data collection. Subscription services employ sophisticated machine learning models that predict churn, forecast spending thresholds, and identify moments of vulnerability or opportunity. These predictive analytics inform everything from personalised pricing tiers to nudges that encourage continued subscription. For example, streaming platforms might time notifications about new releases to coincide with peak user engagement or suggest curated playlists designed to deepen emotional attachment. The business incentives align with keeping users locked in, often at the expense of transparent disclosure or user autonomy.

Insights from former insiders reinforce the depth of these dynamics. Frances Haugen, the Facebook whistleblower, revealed how platforms optimise engagement metrics without adequate regard for user wellbeing. Similarly, Edward Snowden's disclosures on mass data surveillance highlight how data extraction often occurs beyond user awareness or consent. While these cases pertain broadly to digital platforms, the subscription economy shares many of the same structural characteristics: opaque data practices, relentless optimisation for engagement, and prioritisation of revenue over consumer agency.

This reality challenges classical economic notions of a voluntary, transparent marketplace where consumers exercise informed choice. Instead, subscription users frequently encounter *informational asymmetry*—a gap between what they know about how their data is used and what platforms actually do. Consent mechanisms are often opaque or bundled into lengthy terms of service, rendering users unaware of the full extent of data commodification. This imbalance undermines meaningful choice, raising ethical questions about autonomy, privacy, and exploitation in the subscription context.

Moreover, the framing of users as customers is a strategic façade. Marketing materials emphasise personalisation and empowerment, cultivating a sense of control and satisfaction. Yet this narrative masks the reality that consumers' attention and behaviour are meticulously engineered to maximise platform profit. The illusion of bespoke service obscures the fact that engagement metrics and data monetisation drive product design. This tension reveals a profound dissonance between user experience and underlying economic imperatives.

Real-world examples bring this tension into sharp relief. Consider popular fitness apps that offer personalised workout plans while simultaneously collecting granular health and behavioural data. While users may feel empowered and supported, their data fuels targeted advertising and subscription upselling, creating a feedback loop that benefits the platform financially. Similarly, media streaming services curate content libraries to maximise watch time, using behavioural data to predict and shape user preferences, often nudging subscribers toward costly premium tiers or additional offerings.

The implications for consumer agency are significant. Awareness of one's role as a product can provoke discomfort but is crucial for reclaiming autonomy. Users who understand data extraction and behavioural prediction are better equipped to critically evaluate subscription offerings, negotiate privacy settings, and make informed decisions about service value. This understanding also supports advocacy for stronger regulatory frameworks that mandate transparency, data minimisation, and user control.

Ethically, the commodification of subscription users demands scrutiny of platform responsibilities. Business models that prioritise data harvesting and engagement optimisation must be balanced against commitments to user dignity, privacy, and consent. Industry leaders and policymakers increasingly debate frameworks for *data ethics* and *platform accountability*, seeking to align technological innovation with human rights and public interest.

For readers, this chapter offers both a critical lens and practical insights. It encourages a mindset shift from passive consumption to informed participation, fostering vigilance about the unseen economic forces shaping subscription experiences. By illuminating how subscription models transform users into products, it empowers readers to navigate the subscription economy with clarity and intentionality, safeguarding both financial resources and personal sovereignty.

Ultimately, recognising that *you are not the customer, but the product* is not a call for cynicism but for critical engagement. It challenges us to interrogate the design and incentives of subscription platforms, to demand transparency, and to cultivate informed, autonomous relationships with the services that permeate our lives. This insight is foundational to reclaiming agency in a digital economy increasingly predicated on the commodification of human behaviour.

The Rentier Future

The economic landscape is undergoing a profound transformation: a shift from ownership to access as the dominant mode of consumption and wealth extraction. This *rentier future* is not confined to digital media subscriptions or software-as-a-service models but extends deeply into fundamental sectors such as housing, transportation, and education. Where previous generations accumulated assets, property, or durable goods, contemporary economies increasingly monetise perpetual access—turning what was once owned outright into ongoing financial obligations. This structural shift carries profound implications for economic power, social equity, and personal autonomy, demanding critical examination beyond surface-level convenience or innovation.

At its core, the rentier model revolves around the principle that *control over access*, rather than outright ownership, generates sustained revenue streams. Companies and institutions lease, license, or subscriptionise goods and services, ensuring continual payment rather than one-time purchase. This approach recalibrates economic relations, favouring entities that own or mediate access as they collect recurring rents from users. In media and entertainment, streaming platforms replaced physical media sales with monthly fees, capturing steady income tied to ongoing consumption. Yet this paradigm has extended far beyond, infiltrating housing markets through short-term rental platforms, transportation via vehicle and ride-sharing subscriptions, and education through online learning memberships.

Housing exemplifies the rentier future's paradoxical dynamics. Traditional homeownership, long viewed as a cornerstone of economic security and social mobility, faces erosion amid rising property prices, regulatory constraints, and platform-mediated rentals. Companies such as Airbnb have commodified residential spaces into transient assets, while institutional investors increasingly acquire rental properties, shifting wealth accumulation from occupants to landlords and financial intermediaries. Concurrently, subscription-based co-living arrangements and short-term leases offer flexibility but also embed tenants in perpetual payment cycles without equity building. This trend challenges the notion of housing as a right or a stake in community, instead positioning it as a service that demands continuous financial commitment.

Transportation too reflects this reconfiguration. Car ownership—historically a symbol of freedom and status—is giving way to access models like car-sharing, ride-hailing, and subscription services for vehicles. These models promise cost-efficiency and environmental benefits but simultaneously entrench users in ongoing payments that replace the security of owning an asset. The shift reallocates control to service providers who determine pricing, availability, and terms, often through opaque algorithms. This reallocation of agency influences not only personal mobility but broader urban dynamics, raising questions about accessibility, sustainability, and socioeconomic inclusion.

Education's move toward subscription and platform models illustrates the rentier future's reach into human capital formation. Massive open online courses (MOOCs), digital learning subscriptions, and micro-credentialing platforms have disrupted traditional education's ownership model—degrees or certificates earned after fixed terms—in favour of continuous access to content and services. While this promises lifelong learning opportunities, it also fragments credentialing and can create dependency on costly platforms for career advancement. The commodification of knowledge access exacerbates educational inequalities, privileging those who can sustain subscriptions over time.

These shifts cannot be disentangled from broader economic and political trends. The rentier future is intertwined with financialisation—the growing dominance of financial actors and logics over economies—where income derives increasingly from ownership or control of assets rather than productive activity. It echoes historical patterns of rent-seeking, where wealth is accrued by monopolising scarce resources or access rights. Yet today's digital and subscription economies amplify this logic, embedding rentier dynamics within everyday consumption and blurring lines between necessity and luxury.

Critically, the rentier future challenges classical liberal ideals of property, freedom, and economic participation. Ownership traditionally conferred autonomy, security, and generational wealth transfer. Access, while flexible, often entails precarity, recurring costs, and diminished control. This shift exacerbates inequalities as wealth concentrates in the hands of access providers and platforms, while users exchange ownership for ephemeral usage. The social fabric frays as long-term investment in communities and assets declines, replaced by transactional relationships mediated by subscription contracts and digital platforms.

Yet this transformation is not without contestation or complexity. Advocates argue that access models democratise consumption, reduce waste, and foster innovation. Flexibility and affordability purportedly benefit consumers who eschew ownership burdens. Subscription and sharing models can lower entry barriers, allowing broader participation in goods and services. The challenge lies in balancing these benefits with safeguards against exploitation, loss of agency, and systemic inequality.

Navigating the rentier future requires critical financial literacy and policy innovation. Consumers must cultivate awareness of the long-term costs and implications of perpetual access models, recognising how cumulative payments may exceed ownership costs and erode financial independence. Tools for tracking subscription commitments, assessing value, and negotiating terms become essential. Policymakers face the task of regulating subscription markets to ensure transparency, fairness, and protection of user rights, while fostering inclusive access to essential services.

Philosophically, the rentier future invites reflection on the meaning of ownership and the nature of economic freedom in a digitised world. It challenges individuals and societies to reconsider the relationships between possession, use, and identity, and to envision economic arrangements that reconcile flexibility with stability, innovation with equity.

This chapter offers an in-depth analysis of how the economy's pivot from ownership to access is reshaping financial realities and social relations. By dissecting sectoral examples and theoretical frameworks, it equips readers to critically engage with the rentier future—recognising its promises, perils, and possibilities—and to make informed choices within a landscape where access increasingly defines wealth and power.

The Eternal Paywall

The digital revolution promised unprecedented access to knowledge, entertainment, and self-improvement—ideals once celebrated as democratizing forces of the information age. Yet, as subscription models proliferate across cultural and educational domains, an insidious barrier has emerged: the *eternal paywall.* Far from being gateways to open access, these paywalls increasingly fragment and privatise essential resources, locking them behind recurring fees that stratify society and commodify human aspiration. This chapter offers a critical examination of how subscription-based enclosures shape who benefits, who is excluded, and what this means for culture, equity, and individual flourishing.

At the centre of this transformation is the gradual erosion of free or affordable access to knowledge. Once freely available through public libraries, educational institutions, and open platforms, a growing proportion of learning materials, research, and cultural content now reside behind subscription services. Academic publishing exemplifies this shift: paywalled journals and databases place vital scientific and scholarly knowledge beyond the reach of many, including students, independent researchers, and practitioners in resource-constrained environments. This stratification of knowledge access undermines the ethos of collective progress and widens existing educational inequalities, privileging those affiliated with well-funded institutions or affluent networks.

Entertainment, a sector that once relied on ownership of physical media and one-time purchases, has been similarly subsumed under perpetual paywalls. Streaming services dominate cultural consumption, bundling vast libraries into monthly fees. While this promises convenience and variety, it also fractures the cultural commons into proprietary silos. Consumers face escalating costs as content exclusivity drives multiple subscriptions, each granting limited access. The resulting fragmentation not only burdens wallets but reshapes cultural experience, fostering loyalty to platforms over content and challenging shared cultural reference points.

Self-improvement, a domain traditionally accessible through community resources, workshops, or self-directed study, has also been commodified. Subscription-based wellness apps, online coaching, and curated personal development platforms offer tailored pathways to growth but at a financial premium. The reliance on continuous payment for access transforms self-improvement into a service contingent on sustained affordability, creating potential dependencies and excluding those unable to participate fully. This commodification raises questions about the authenticity and inclusivity of personal development in a subscription-saturated culture.

Who profits from this proliferation of paywalls is clear: corporations, platform owners, and shareholders extract recurring revenues from captive audiences, maximising lifetime value through subscription inertia and algorithmically optimised retention. These entities leverage data and behavioural insights to refine offerings, personalise upsells, and limit cancellation friction, embedding consumers in ongoing financial commitments. The consolidation of cultural and educational assets under powerful platform monopolies raises concerns about market concentration, content diversity, and cultural autonomy.

Conversely, those who lose are often less visible but deeply affected: low-income individuals, independent creators, students in underserved regions, and the culturally marginalised. The fracturing of access exacerbates social divides, limiting participation in knowledge economies and cultural dialogues. It also pressures individuals into managing multiple subscriptions, often at the cost of other essential needs, fostering financial stress and exclusion.

Critically, this situation invites reflection on the ethical and social responsibilities of subscription providers. The enclosure of knowledge and culture through paywalls challenges the notion of information as a public good. It compels reconsideration of business models that balance profitability with equitable access, transparency, and cultural stewardship. Emerging initiatives such as open-access publishing, nonprofit streaming platforms, and subsidised educational subscriptions offer alternative visions but face structural and financial hurdles.

Culturally, the eternal paywall shifts not only access but also agency and identity. The act of subscribing becomes a signal of belonging and capacity, entwining financial status with cultural participation. This dynamic redefines who is included in contemporary knowledge and cultural conversations, potentially narrowing diversity of thought and experience. It also shapes consumer behaviour, privileging passive reception of curated content over active creation and critical engagement.

Navigating the era of the eternal paywall demands heightened consumer literacy and advocacy. Individuals benefit from tools that illuminate cumulative subscription costs, encourage critical evaluation of value, and promote intentional curation of access. Simultaneously, collective action—through policy reform, institutional innovation, and cultural movements—is necessary to challenge monopolistic enclosure and foster more inclusive models.

This chapter dissects the complex interplay of economics, culture, and technology that underpins the rise of subscription paywalls across vital domains. It equips readers with the analytical framework to understand who benefits and who suffers from this shift, and the conceptual tools to envision a more equitable and accessible future for knowledge, entertainment, and self-improvement. In doing so, it asserts that access to culture and education is not merely a commodity but a foundational element of a just and flourishing society.

Financial Servitude by Design

Subscription contracts, with their promise of convenience and continuity, often appear as benign financial arrangements—modern tools designed for effortless access to goods and services. Yet beneath their polished interfaces and seamless user experiences lies a deeper and more troubling parallel: these *subscription traps* echo historical forms of financial servitude, drawing uncomfortable lines to systems like indentured labour that ensnared individuals in cycles of dependence and restricted freedom. By framing recurring revenue structures as morally neutral or purely transactional, society overlooks how these mechanisms can perpetuate subtle but persistent forms of economic bondage, demanding a critical reassessment of their ethical and social implications.

Indentured servitude, a widespread practice from the seventeenth to the nineteenth centuries, involved contractual agreements where individuals exchanged years of labour for passage, housing, or basic subsistence. While ostensibly voluntary, these contracts often trapped workers in exploitative cycles marked by limited agency, onerous obligations, and legal constraints on exit. Analogously, modern subscription contracts can impose financial and psychological constraints that mimic servitude in a digital economy. Though less overtly coercive, their design frequently discourages cancellation, obfuscates cumulative costs, and fosters inertia, binding consumers into prolonged commitments that outlast the initial perceived value.

A key mechanism enabling this modern servitude is the *subscription trap*—a contractual and psychological snare that exploits behavioural biases such as loss aversion, sunk cost fallacy, and decision fatigue. Users, enticed by free trials or low introductory rates, may find themselves locked into automatic renewals with complicated cancellation processes. Over time, the aggregate cost and reduced satisfaction create a paradox: consumers feel trapped yet rationalise ongoing payments to avoid perceived losses or administrative hassle. This dynamic erodes financial autonomy, mirroring the lack of exit options that characterised historical indenture.

Legal frameworks governing subscriptions often compound this issue. Terms of service tend to be dense, complex, and skewed in favour of providers, limiting consumer recourse and transparency. The absence of standardised protections or mandated disclosures leaves many users unaware of their rights or the true financial implications. This legal opacity parallels the limited agency historically experienced by indentured individuals bound by rigid contracts and enforcement mechanisms. In both cases, power asymmetries favour the entity controlling access or service provision, perpetuating economic dependency under the guise of voluntary exchange.

Ethically, the moral neutrality often attributed to recurring revenue models warrants scrutiny. Viewing subscription contracts as mere market transactions ignores their embedded social and psychological dimensions. The convenience and perceived value they offer must be balanced against the potential for exploitation and harm, particularly among vulnerable populations who may be disproportionately affected by financial inertia or limited literacy. This tension raises questions about corporate responsibility, consumer protection, and the role of regulation in safeguarding autonomy within a subscription economy.

Real-world examples illustrate the depth of these dynamics. Consider telecommunications and digital content providers who structure pricing and renewal policies to maximise retention, often obscuring cancellation pathways. Consumers locked into multi-year contracts face penalties, limited alternatives, and psychological pressure to continue payments despite dissatisfaction. Similar patterns emerge in fitness memberships, online learning platforms, and meal subscription services, where ongoing charges accumulate quietly, sometimes unbeknownst to users, reflecting a systemic design that prioritises profit over consumer freedom.

Comparative historical analysis enriches understanding by situating subscription servitude within a lineage of economic dependency practices. While modern contracts lack physical coercion or legal indenture's brutality, they replicate core features: binding commitment, constrained exit, and unequal bargaining power. This parallel challenges narratives that celebrate subscription models uncritically as innovative or consumer-friendly, demanding a nuanced perspective attentive to structural inequalities and power asymmetries.

Strategies to counteract subscription servitude by design must be multifaceted. Consumer education that enhances awareness of contract terms, cumulative costs, and behavioural traps is foundational. Policy interventions such as mandated transparency, simplified cancellation procedures, and limits on automatic renewals can restore balance. Moreover, fostering a cultural shift towards critical engagement with subscription models encourages consumers to view recurring payments not as defaults but as active choices requiring ongoing evaluation.

Psychologically, breaking free from subscription servitude involves recognising and resisting cognitive biases that entrench ongoing commitments. Tools that prompt regular auditing of subscriptions, reflective budgeting, and emotional self-awareness empower consumers to reclaim agency. This process aligns with broader financial mindfulness practices that integrate emotional and behavioural insights to promote sustainable money management.

This chapter contends that recurring revenue structures are not morally neutral commercial devices but complex social phenomena with significant implications for autonomy, equity, and dignity. By drawing on historical parallels, contemporary case studies, and ethical analysis, it illuminates how subscription contracts can function as modern instruments of financial servitude. Recognising this reality is critical for individuals seeking freedom within the subscription economy and for societies striving to create fairer, more transparent economic systems.

Ultimately, *financial servitude by design* compels us to rethink the assumptions underpinning subscription culture, challenging both providers and consumers to foster practices and policies that prioritise genuine choice, informed consent, and equitable power relations. It invites a reimagining of recurring revenue not as a trap but as a tool when wielded with responsibility, transparency, and respect for human agency.

Chapter 6
The Anatomy of a Subscription Trap

The subscription economy—so often praised for its ease and adaptability—conceals within it a far more intricate machinery than most realise. What appears as a seamless service, a free trial here, a discounted bundle there, is in fact part of a carefully engineered architecture: the subscription trap. Behind the frictionless sign-up screens lies a system designed not merely to attract but to tether, to convert curiosity into obligation and habit. To see it clearly is to reclaim something vital—our time, attention, and, not least, our financial independence. This chapter sets out to unpick the mechanisms at play, examining how psychological levers and structural barriers combine to sustain loyalty and forestall escape.

The first snare is almost always the onboarding hook. Here the industry deploys its best tricks: free trials that lower suspicion, discounts that generate a false sense of urgency, bundles that make saying "no" feel like leaving money on the table. Streaming platforms, in particular, excel at this choreography. Entry feels smooth, even generous. Exit, by contrast, is where the real game begins. Case studies consistently reveal the same pattern: effortless enrolment paired with deliberate resistance at the point of cancellation. What seems like convenience is, in truth, a design steeped in behavioural economics—loss aversion, commitment bias, default effects—all enlisted to transform tentative users into long-term subscribers with barely a murmur of dissent.

Yet the trap does not stop at the door. The next layer is frictionless retention, which is anything but frictionless when the user attempts to leave. Companies funnel resources into making sign-up near instantaneous, all bright buttons and intuitive swipes, while the path to cancellation is labyrinthine: multiple screens, confirmation prompts, sometimes even a phone call to customer service. Friction, in this context, is no accident. It is a tool. The irritation it breeds is meant to dissuade, to drain resolve. Awareness of this tactic is itself a defence. With preparation, consumers can cut through the tangle—step by step, without the paralysis that such systems are designed to induce.

Then comes loyalty, gamified and glossed with the rhetoric of achievement. Points, badges, tiers, exclusive perks—all carefully constructed to bind not only our wallets but our sense of self. Consider Peloton, with its milestones and digital cheers, or Duolingo, with its streaks and leaderboards. The rewards feel personal, hard-won, almost sacred. Yet, in economic terms, many of these benefits are marginal, even hollow. The deeper question emerges: is this loyalty truly ours, freely offered, or is it manufactured, coaxed into being by clever scaffolding that blurs the line between genuine belonging and engineered dependence?

For those wishing to step outside the cycle, knowledge alone is insufficient; an escape plan is needed. The chapter lays out a "Subscription Exit Strategy"—methodical, not punitive. It begins with an audit: listing every recurring payment and asking not just what it costs, but whether it brings value or joy. From there, a hierarchy is formed, essentials at the top, indulgences further down. The next step anticipates cancellation hurdles, preparing the patience and persistence required. Finally, routines are established to keep financial clarity intact—regular reviews, conscious choices, a rhythm of intentional stewardship. Such practices shift the posture from passive entanglement to deliberate authorship of one's subscription landscape.

Throughout, examples from daily life anchor the analysis: families juggling a half-dozen streaming bills, professionals blindsided by forgotten renewals, students ensnared in "mandatory" learning platforms. These stories illustrate a simple truth: the subscription trap is not incidental but systemic, a fusion of psychology and commerce designed for perpetual engagement.

To dissect its anatomy, as this chapter attempts, is to issue both warning and invitation. The warning: convenience is rarely neutral; it is engineered to serve retention. The invitation: by seeing through the design, consumers can recover agency, choosing consciously rather than drifting in the currents of algorithmic persuasion. The subscription economy may not be vanishing anytime soon, but with vigilance and strategy, it need not dictate the terms of our financial or emotional lives.

The Onboarding Hook

The moment a consumer encounters a subscription service, they step into a carefully choreographed dance designed to convert curiosity into commitment. This initial engagement—what we term the *onboarding hook*—employs an arsenal of psychological and marketing strategies crafted to neutralise skepticism and lower the barriers to entry. Free trials, introductory discounts, bundled offers: these are not mere incentives but calibrated tools that ease users into a state of acceptance, often before they fully grasp the long-term financial and behavioural implications. This subchapter unpacks these common onboarding tricks, revealing their potency and subtlety, while examining their broader consequences through the lens of a compelling case study: streaming services and the paradox of subscription versus cancellation behaviour.

Free trials stand as perhaps the most ubiquitous and effective of onboarding tactics. Presented as risk-free opportunities to "try before you buy," they tap directly into consumers' aversion to loss and desire for certainty. The psychological calculus at play is deceptively simple: if something is free and easy to access, why not engage? Yet, beneath this apparent generosity lies a trap. Trials often require payment details upfront, and their expiration can trigger automatic renewals that shift users seamlessly into paying subscribers. The momentary suspension of financial commitment fosters behavioural inertia, while the effort required to cancel introduces subtle frictions that discourage termination. This dynamic exploits well-documented cognitive biases—default effects and status quo bias—making the trial-to-subscription transition psychologically effortless but financially consequential.

Introductory discounts serve a complementary function. By offering a reduced rate for an initial period, services create a sense of urgency and exceptional value, encouraging rapid sign-up. This pricing strategy leverages the principle of *anchoring*, where consumers compare the discounted fee against the full price and perceive a bargain too good to miss. However, once the promotional period lapses, the price reverts, often catching subscribers unprepared for the increased cost. The psychological discomfort of losing a "deal" leads many to accept the higher fee passively, rationalising continued subscription to avoid regret. Such discounts effectively build subscriber bases while priming consumers for future revenue.

Bundles complicate the onboarding hook by aggregating multiple offerings into a single subscription, enhancing perceived value through quantity and convenience. Streaming services, telecom providers, and software companies commonly employ this strategy to lock consumers into ecosystems that are difficult and costly to leave. The bundling effect also obscures the cost of individual components, reducing price salience and increasing overall spend. By framing bundled subscriptions as comprehensive solutions, companies appeal to the consumer's desire for simplicity and completeness, even as they accumulate incremental financial commitments.

A revealing case study lies in the behaviour of streaming service subscribers, whose engagement typifies the onboarding trap. Research shows that while sign-up rates for free trials and introductory offers are high, cancellation rates during or immediately after these periods remain surprisingly low. Many users, despite limited usage or dissatisfaction, continue paying beyond the trial, influenced by the friction of cancellation processes and the psychological cost of "losing" access. This persistence often contrasts starkly with consumers' stated intentions, highlighting the power of onboarding hooks to override rational decision-making. Industry data indicates that companies actively monitor and optimise these onboarding experiences to maximise conversion, creating a finely tuned system that prioritises retention over transparency.

Critically, these onboarding mechanisms do not operate in isolation but within an ecosystem designed to maximise lifetime customer value. By the time a subscriber moves beyond onboarding, the groundwork for long-term engagement—and financial commitment—has been firmly laid. This raises ethical considerations about the balance between effective marketing and consumer manipulation. While companies argue that free trials and discounts democratise access and reduce risk, critics contend that these strategies exploit cognitive vulnerabilities and obscure the true costs of subscription.

The nuanced psychology underpinning the onboarding hook also invites reflection on consumer agency and informed consent. The opacity of terms and conditions, combined with subtle design choices that prioritise enrolment over exit, creates an environment where genuine consent is compromised. Consumers often underestimate the ease with which trials convert to paid subscriptions or the effort required to cancel, leading to frustration and financial strain. Addressing this disconnect requires transparency reforms, clearer communication, and streamlined cancellation processes that restore balance in the subscription relationship.

For readers seeking to navigate the onboarding hook with awareness, this chapter offers practical insights and critical frameworks. Understanding the psychological levers at play empowers consumers to approach free trials, discounts, and bundles with informed skepticism rather than passive acquiescence. Recognising the tension between convenience and commitment fosters a mindset equipped to interrogate the true costs and benefits of subscription entry points.

In sum, the onboarding hook is a sophisticated architecture of persuasion, finely calibrated to lower defences and secure subscription commitments. By dissecting its components and effects, this chapter illuminates how initial engagement strategies shape long-term financial and behavioural patterns, offering readers the clarity and tools needed to reclaim agency in a subscription economy engineered for seamless enrolment but challenging exit.

Frictionless Retention

Subscription services masterfully engineer an experience where signing up is effortless, but exiting is often fraught with obstacles. This deliberate design—*frictionless entry paired with friction-loaded cancellation*—lies at the core of what might be called *frictionless retention.* By smoothing the path into subscription commitments while erecting barriers against termination, companies secure prolonged customer engagement and revenue streams, often at the expense of consumer autonomy. Understanding this asymmetry is crucial for anyone seeking to navigate the subscription economy with intention and regain control over their financial commitments.

The allure of frictionless entry is intuitive: users can sign up with minimal effort, often completing the process in just a few clicks or taps. Free trials, one-click subscriptions, and pre-filled payment information facilitate rapid onboarding, encouraging impulse decisions and reducing cognitive resistance. This design leverages well-known psychological principles such as the *path of least resistance* and *immediacy bias*, where consumers favour immediate gratification and simple processes over deliberation and effort. By eliminating friction at the start, companies maximise conversion rates, drawing users into a commitment before fully contemplating its long-term consequences.

In stark contrast, cancellation processes are frequently labyrinthine, opaque, and time-consuming. Users may be required to navigate multiple pages, select from convoluted menus, endure repeated confirmation prompts, or even speak to customer service representatives—often trained to persuade retention. This *exit friction* capitalises on behavioural economics insights like *loss aversion* and *status quo bias*, where the effort and discomfort associated with cancellation deter many from following through. The resulting inertia not only inflates subscriber counts artificially but also generates resentment and financial drain, as users remain bound to services that no longer serve them.

Consider the case of major streaming platforms. While signing up for a trial or discounted subscription is swift and seamless, cancellation often involves navigating a maze of account settings, re-entering passwords, and confirming cancellation multiple times. Industry analyses reveal that a significant proportion of subscribers never complete the cancellation process, either deterred by the complexity or unaware that their subscription has renewed automatically. This disparity in friction directly translates into sustained revenue and illustrates the power imbalance between consumers and providers.

The ethical dimensions of frictionless retention warrant serious consideration. While convenience at sign-up benefits consumers, the deliberate creation of barriers to cancellation can be seen as exploitative, undermining informed consent and autonomy. It raises questions about the moral responsibilities of companies to design transparent, fair, and user-centric experiences. Calls for regulatory intervention—mandating simple, immediate cancellation options and clear communication about subscription terms—reflect growing awareness of this issue and its societal impact.

Practical strategies empower consumers to push through cancellation friction and reclaim agency. Awareness is the first step: recognising that friction exists by design equips users to anticipate and prepare for it. Documenting cancellation policies, setting calendar reminders before trial expirations, and compiling all necessary account information reduce procedural barriers. Cultivating a mindset that views cancellation as an act of financial self-care rather than inconvenience helps overcome emotional resistance. Sharing cancellation experiences in online communities or with trusted peers can also provide social support and practical tips.

Technology itself can assist in managing friction. Subscription tracking apps and browser extensions alert users to upcoming renewals and simplify account management. These tools reduce the cognitive load of monitoring multiple subscriptions and lower the threshold for timely cancellations. However, reliance on third-party tools introduces new considerations around privacy and security, requiring careful selection and awareness.

Frictionless retention also intersects with broader behavioural patterns. Consumers often underestimate the cumulative financial impact of lingering subscriptions, while emotional attachments to services or identity associations (such as "I'm a subscriber of X") reinforce continuation despite diminished value. Understanding these psychological dynamics complements procedural strategies, enabling a holistic approach to escaping subscription traps.

Companies justify streamlined sign-up and layered cancellation procedures as business necessities—balancing user convenience with retention metrics vital for growth and investor confidence. Yet this balance often skews toward the latter, prioritising revenue over customer experience. Transparent dialogue about these trade-offs and consumer empowerment can foster more ethical subscription ecosystems.

Ultimately, frictionless retention exemplifies how design choices shape economic power relations in the subscription economy. By dissecting these dynamics and providing actionable insights, this chapter equips readers to identify, confront, and overcome friction barriers. It invites a shift from passive acceptance to active stewardship of subscriptions, fostering financial sovereignty in a marketplace engineered for perpetual engagement.

Gamified Loyalty, Hollow Value

Loyalty programs and engagement-based subscriptions have become ubiquitous features of the modern consumer landscape, promising rewards, status, and personalised experiences in exchange for continued patronage. From airline frequent flyer miles and supermarket points to Peloton's fitness challenges and Duolingo's streaks, these systems offer a seductive blend of gratification and belonging. Yet beneath this veneer of goodwill and mutual benefit lies a more complex reality: loyalty is not merely freely given but often meticulously engineered, leveraging gamification and behavioural science to create a sense of attachment that may be disproportionate to the actual value provided. This subchapter interrogates the mechanics and implications of gamified loyalty, questioning whether the value conferred is substantive or hollow and what this means for consumer autonomy and corporate power.

At its core, gamification adapts game-design elements—points, levels, badges, leaderboards, and rewards—to non-game contexts, aiming to motivate participation, increase engagement, and shape behaviour. In subscription models, gamification fosters habitual use and emotional investment, transforming routine consumption into a performance or challenge. Peloton, for example, offers real-time metrics, virtual high-fives, and competitive rankings, turning exercise into a communal, interactive event. Duolingo capitalises on daily streaks and achievement badges to encourage language learning persistence. These features generate dopamine responses akin to those found in gaming, reinforcing continued engagement through intermittent rewards and social validation.

However, the economic value of these loyalty programs often pales beside the psychological investment they demand. Points accumulated may be difficult to redeem, subject to expiry, or available only for restricted goods and services, rendering them less tangible than they appear. The promise of "free" rewards masks the reality that such systems are engineered to keep consumers spending more and staying subscribed longer, with the reward mechanisms serving as incentives to avoid cancellation or lapse. This disjunction between perceived and actual value has prompted criticism that gamified loyalty systems create *hollow value*—a veneer of benefit that primarily serves corporate retention objectives rather than genuine consumer enrichment.

Moreover, the engineered nature of loyalty raises profound ethical questions about consumer consent and manipulation. When companies deploy behavioural design techniques that exploit cognitive biases such as loss aversion, commitment consistency, and social proof, the line between voluntary engagement and coerced attachment blurs. The experience of loyalty becomes less about authentic preference and more about navigating psychological traps crafted to prolong subscription and expenditure. This dynamic undermines the traditional notion of loyalty as an earned, reciprocal relationship grounded in trust and value exchange.

Real-world examples illuminate this tension. Studies reveal that while loyalty programs can increase short-term spending, they often do so by incentivising unnecessary purchases or prolonging subscriptions beyond actual user satisfaction. For instance, consumers may continue renewing a streaming service primarily to preserve accumulated "watch credits" or exclusive perks rather than out of genuine interest. Similarly, fitness app users may push through physical or emotional discomfort to maintain streaks or rankings, conflating gamified achievements with personal progress. These behaviours highlight how gamified loyalty can distort consumer priorities and obscure critical assessment of value.

The gamification of loyalty also intersects with identity and social belonging, intensifying its hold. Subscribers may internalise platform engagement as part of their self-concept, identifying as "Peloton riders" or "Duolingo learners," which deepens emotional bonds and complicates disengagement. The communal aspects—leaderboards, social groups, shared challenges—amplify this effect by embedding users within networked social validation loops. Here, loyalty extends beyond financial transaction into realms of identity and affiliation, raising questions about autonomy and the commodification of social connection.

Yet, it is important to recognise the dual-edged nature of gamified loyalty. When thoughtfully designed and ethically implemented, these systems can enhance user experience, provide meaningful motivation, and build supportive communities. They may democratise access to fitness, education, and culture by making engagement enjoyable and accessible. The challenge lies in balancing motivational design with transparency, fairness, and respect for user autonomy—ensuring that loyalty emerges from authentic value rather than engineered dependency.

For consumers, cultivating awareness of gamification's psychological mechanisms is vital. Critical engagement involves recognising how points, badges, and perks influence behaviour and questioning whether continued participation aligns with genuine needs and values. Developing a reflective approach to subscription loyalty can mitigate susceptibility to hollow value traps and empower intentional decision-making. Strategies include periodic reassessment of subscription benefits, mindful disengagement from addictive reward cycles, and prioritising services that offer clear, substantive value.

From a broader perspective, policymakers and consumer advocates face the task of scrutinising gamified loyalty within subscription economies. Regulatory frameworks might demand clearer disclosures about reward program terms, guard against manipulative design practices, and encourage alternatives that prioritise consumer welfare. Public discourse on the ethics of behavioural design in commerce is essential to foster more equitable and transparent subscription models.

In sum, *gamified loyalty* represents a potent, yet ambivalent force in contemporary subscription culture. By deconstructing its psychological architecture and economic realities, this chapter reveals how loyalty is often less an organic choice and more a cultivated state, engineered through game mechanics that reward engagement while concealing hollow value. Understanding these dynamics equips readers to navigate subscription ecosystems with critical insight, preserve their financial and emotional autonomy, and foster authentic relationships with the services they choose to support.

Escape Protocols

Escaping the subscription trap often feels like an uphill battle: the convenience that drew us in now conceals a tangle of auto-renewals, obscure cancellation processes, and psychological barriers that sap our attention and resources. Yet, liberation is not only possible—it can be achieved systematically, without overwhelm or guilt. This subchapter offers a powerful, step-by-step *Subscription Exit Strategy* designed to help readers reclaim both their capital and cognitive bandwidth, empowering them to disengage thoughtfully, efficiently, and sustainably from unwanted or underutilised subscriptions.

The first step in this strategy is *comprehensive auditing.* Awareness is the cornerstone of change, and many subscribers remain unaware of the full scope of their commitments. By methodically cataloguing every recurring payment—across bank statements, credit card records, and email confirmations—individuals gain a clear map of their subscription landscape. This exercise reveals not only direct costs but also the hidden cumulative drain on finances. Importantly, it uncovers forgotten or duplicate subscriptions that quietly erode budgets. Real-world examples highlight how such audits have led to surprising discoveries, sometimes uncovering hundreds of pounds in dormant charges. This transparency catalyses accountability and prioritises exit efforts.

Following auditing, the strategy moves to *value assessment.* Not all subscriptions carry equal weight in terms of utility, joy, or necessity. Assigning criteria—such as frequency of use, alignment with personal values, and cost-benefit ratio—enables prioritisation. This reflective step invites readers to question emotional attachments, habitual spending, and rationalisations like "I might use it someday." Cognitive behavioural insights suggest that confronting these narratives with objective data dismantles inertia. Case studies illustrate families who halved their subscription expenses simply by clarifying which services genuinely enhanced their lives versus those that lingered from past impulses or social pressures.

The next phase addresses the *cancellation process* itself, often the most daunting obstacle. This step entails gathering detailed information on cancellation procedures, required credentials, and timelines to avoid unwanted renewals. Preparation involves setting calendar reminders for trial expirations and noting customer service contacts if manual intervention is necessary. Recognising that companies intentionally design cancellation flows to introduce friction, the strategy advocates persistence and strategic navigation. Drawing on behavioural research, it encourages readers to reframe cancellation not as an inconvenience but as an act of financial self-care. Success stories abound of subscribers who overcame complex hurdles through perseverance and systematic approaches.

Parallel to procedural tactics, the exit strategy emphasises *mindset shifts* vital for sustainable disengagement. Letting go of subscriptions often triggers emotional responses—guilt, fear of missing out, or shame over perceived failure. Cultivating self-compassion and reframing financial autonomy as empowerment mitigates these feelings. Practices such as journaling about motivations, sharing intentions with trusted confidantes, or seeking support in community groups foster psychological resilience. This dimension transforms the exit from a transactional event into a meaningful act of reclaiming control and aligning spending with authentic priorities.

Technology offers supplementary tools that complement human effort. Subscription management apps and digital wallets can automate auditing, alert users to upcoming charges, and simplify cancellation steps. However, reliance on such tools must be balanced with vigilance regarding privacy and data security. Educated consumers critically evaluate these aids, integrating them judiciously into a broader strategy rather than delegating agency.

Importantly, the exit strategy advocates *gradual disengagement* where appropriate, avoiding abrupt all-or-nothing approaches that risk burnout or relapse. Phased cancellation—starting with least valuable or most costly services—builds confidence and momentum. This measured approach respects behavioural tendencies towards change and reduces psychological resistance. Evidence from behavioural economics supports incremental adjustment as more effective than radical overhaul for lasting financial behaviour change.

Beyond individual tactics, the strategy encourages *ongoing subscription stewardship*. Exiting is not a one-off event but part of a continuous practice of intentional spending. Regular review intervals—quarterly or biannually—maintain awareness and prevent accumulation of unwanted subscriptions. Embedding budgeting within a narrative framework that connects spending to values and goals ensures alignment over time. This perspective fosters financial mindfulness and guards against relapse into passive, automatic renewal patterns.

Ethical reflections permeate this strategy. Navigating subscription exits is not merely a personal finance exercise but an act of resistance against opaque, friction-heavy corporate practices. Recognising the systemic nature of subscription traps underscores the importance of collective advocacy for transparency, fair cancellation policies, and consumer rights protections. Empowered individuals, equipped with exit protocols, can become agents of change, demanding better standards and fostering market accountability.

This comprehensive Subscription Exit Strategy thus balances pragmatic steps with psychological insight, technological aids, and ethical awareness. It transforms a daunting challenge into a structured, manageable process that respects human complexity and honours personal sovereignty. Readers are invited to approach their subscriptions not as passive recipients but as active curators, choosing engagement deliberately and exiting decisively. Through this empowered stewardship, they reclaim not just money and attention, but autonomy and clarity in a subscription-saturated world.

Chapter 7
Budgeting as Ethical Practice

For too long, budgeting has been imagined as little more than a cold exercise in arithmetic: tally your income, subtract your expenses, put aside a portion for savings. Numbers stacked neatly in rows, percentages marching across the page. But beneath that supposed neutrality lies something more provocative—a moral terrain. Every financial decision carries echoes, reverberating through social fabrics, environmental systems, cultural narratives. And in an age dominated by subscriptions—those quiet monthly charges that drip-feed entire industries—the act of budgeting is no longer merely managerial. It becomes, whether we admit it or not, an ethical stance, a declaration of what we choose to sustain and what we allow to wither.

"Every pound is a vote." The phrase may sound glib at first, but its truth deepens upon reflection. With a subscription, unlike a one-off purchase, our "vote" repeats month after month, affirming the structures and practices we underwrite. It is not unusual for consumers to find themselves, by a kind of financial autopilot, funding enterprises whose ethos sits uneasily with their own—be it a streaming platform that mines personal data, or a delivery service built upon precarious gig labour. In this light, the budget ceases to be a ledger of private convenience. It becomes dialogue—often unspoken—with corporations, with governments, with society at large. The question is no longer only "can I afford this?" but "what am I endorsing by affording it?"

This lens of ethics sharpens further when turned toward the environment. Consider the hidden cost of convenience: the electricity hungry data centres that keep streaming platforms alive, the layers of packaging that cushion every on-demand delivery, the relentless churn of updates and upgrades, each demanding energy and raw materials. The cumulative weight of these habits strains the planet, yet traditional budgeting discussions rarely count such costs. To budget with sustainability in mind is to widen the scope, to see the ecological shadow of one's subscriptions. The challenge—and opportunity—lies in choosing differently: consolidating services, selecting providers with genuine environmental commitments, or simply consuming less. Convenience need not vanish; it can, instead, be redefined.

From here, the chapter advances a framework it calls "value-to-values" alignment. The phrase is more than wordplay; it is a method for interrogating whether our spending reflects, or betrays, our convictions. What does it mean, for instance, to cherish community yet bankroll companies that hollow it out? Or to profess care for the earth while fuelling industries that ravage it? By auditing subscriptions through this ethical prism, readers are invited not to wallow in guilt but to disengage deliberately, pruning away the dissonant and nurturing the congruent. The point is less about renunciation than about coherence—aligning money with meaning.

Yet no exploration of ethical budgeting can sidestep capitalism's paradoxes. How, after all, does one resist while participating? Is complicity inevitable? The chapter does not pretend easy answers. Instead, it draws upon critical theory, contemporary philosophy, and lived practice to propose tools for navigating these tensions. Terms such as "mindful capitalism" or "radical responsibility" are not panaceas but provocations—ways of thinking about the self as both actor and acted upon. Budgeting, seen through this lens, resembles less a technical chore than an ongoing practice of identity. A spiritual discipline, even. Each choice—subscribe, cancel, renew—becomes part of a dialogue between the individual's freedom and the system's gravity.

Woven through the analysis are real examples: households who consciously redirect their budgets towards cooperatives, activists who treat subscription audits as acts of protest, communities pooling resources to underwrite sustainable alternatives. Their stories illustrate both the potency and the limitations of individual action. No budget, however intentional, can by itself reform unjust structures. Yet personal commitment, multiplied across many, has historically seeded collective change.

What emerges, then, is a call to see budgeting as more than balance sheets. It is a practice of citizenship—messy, imperfect, but deeply consequential. Each recurring charge is a thread in the tapestry of economy and culture. To track it, to question it, is to participate in shaping the world those threads weave.

In the end, this chapter argues for a shift: from passive management to mindful stewardship, from transactions to conscience. Budgeting, so reframed, becomes a means not only to secure personal clarity but to contribute deliberately to the shared future. It asks us to wield financial power with intention, to steady ourselves against the swirl of consumption, and to craft a relationship with money that honours both our values and our vision of what life ought to be.

Every Dollar is a Vote

Every financial decision, no matter how seemingly trivial, carries with it a profound ethical weight. The old adage that *"money talks"* extends far beyond the transactional realm, reaching into the structures and values that shape society. In the context of the subscription economy—where small, repeated charges silently accumulate—each payment functions not just as a transfer of funds, but as a continuous endorsement of the institutions and industries we support. To budget with this awareness is to engage in a form of ethical activism, where *every dollar is a vote* cast for the world we wish to inhabit. This subchapter invites readers to explore this pivotal shift in perspective, revealing how recurring charges underpin systems that may contradict personal values and offering a roadmap to more conscious financial participation.

At first glance, the act of paying a subscription fee can feel routine or mechanical—an automatic deduction from a bank account that rarely prompts reflection. Yet, this automation obscures the powerful signals embedded within these payments. Whether a streaming platform, a news outlet, a social media service, or a consumer goods delivery, each subscription injects capital into entities whose policies, labour practices, and cultural impact reverberate widely. For example, recent investigations have exposed how some media subscriptions funnel revenue into conglomerates that influence political discourse or censor dissenting voices. Similarly, food delivery services, while convenient, often perpetuate precarious working conditions for couriers. These realities underscore the ethical dimension lurking beneath the surface of subscription billing statements.

The concept of budgeting as ethical activism emerges from this recognition. It challenges the reductive view of budgeting as mere expense management and reframes it as an act of deliberate value expression. Subscribers become voters in a marketplace of ideas, labour standards, and environmental footprints. Their financial commitments can reinforce or resist dominant systems, making the act of choosing subscriptions an extension of civic engagement. This perspective elevates financial literacy to ethical literacy, encouraging consumers to scrutinise not only prices and features but also the social and political consequences of their spending.

Concrete examples illustrate how this dynamic plays out. Consider the rise of streaming services with diverse corporate ownerships. A subscriber who selects a platform solely for its content might be unaware that their payments contribute to advertising algorithms that manipulate viewer preferences or to data practices that compromise privacy. Alternatively, opting for a smaller, independent provider may align spending with values of decentralisation and data ethics, even if the service is less polished or more costly. These choices exemplify how budgeting decisions ripple beyond individual utility into broader societal impacts.

Moreover, subscription models often entrench patterns of passive consumption, where convenience supersedes scrutiny. Auto-renewals and bundled services blur the lines between conscious support and inadvertent complicity. Ethical budgeting demands breaking this passivity through regular audits and intentional reflection, uncovering subscriptions that may no longer serve or align with one's evolving values. This practice transforms budgeting into a living dialogue—between one's financial realities, ethical commitments, and aspirations for change.

The tension between consumer power and corporate influence remains complex. On one hand, individual subscriptions aggregate into significant economic flows that can shift markets and incentivise reform. On the other, systemic inequalities and monopolistic practices limit the range of ethical choices available, raising questions about the efficacy of individual activism within entrenched capitalist structures. This subchapter does not shy away from these contradictions but situates them within a nuanced framework that recognises both the potential and the limits of ethical budgeting.

Furthermore, engaging with budgeting as ethical activism opens avenues for collective action. Consumer coalitions, subscription boycotts, and transparency campaigns have successfully pressured companies to adopt fairer practices and environmental standards. In this light, budgeting transcends private management and enters the public sphere, where aggregated choices influence corporate behaviour and policy debates. Readers are encouraged to view their financial decisions as part of a larger ecosystem of activism, amplifying their impact through community and advocacy.

Philosophically, repositioning budgeting as voting challenges deeply ingrained notions about money and morality. It disrupts the separation of economic life from ethical reflection, insisting that financial behaviour is inseparable from one's identity and responsibility as a member of society. This holistic approach resonates with contemporary movements for conscious capitalism and social justice, advocating for an economy that serves human and planetary wellbeing rather than abstract profit maximisation.

Practically, the chapter equips readers with tools to enact this paradigm shift. It guides them in mapping subscriptions against their ethical priorities, researching corporate practices, and making informed decisions about continuance or cancellation. It also highlights the importance of transparency and accountability, urging consumers to demand clearer information about where their recurring payments go and what values they support. These steps empower readers to reclaim agency in a financial environment often characterised by opacity and inertia.

By illuminating how *every dollar is a vote*, this exploration reframes budgeting from a technical chore into a dynamic practice of ethical engagement. It invites readers to become discerning voters in economic life, recognising that the cumulative effect of their subscription choices contributes to shaping industries, cultures, and futures. This perspective fosters not only financial mindfulness but also a deepened sense of moral clarity and purposeful participation in the world.

The Environmental Cost of Convenience

The allure of convenience has become one of the defining features of contemporary life. From instant streaming of films and music to doorstep delivery of groceries and consumer goods, the subscription economy promises effortless access to almost anything, whenever it is wanted. Yet this ease of consumption conceals an escalating environmental toll, one that remains largely invisible to most consumers. The ecological cost of constant digital delivery—across media, food, and goods—raises urgent questions about sustainability in an economy structured around immediacy and perpetual renewal. This subchapter undertakes a rigorous investigation of these hidden impacts, urging readers to rethink their subscription choices through an ecological lens and embrace more sustainable practices.

At the heart of this issue lies the growing scale and frequency of delivery services. The convenience of food delivery apps, for example, has transformed urban eating habits, generating a surge in packaging waste and transportation emissions. Studies estimate that meal delivery contributes significantly to urban carbon footprints, not only because of the vehicles involved but also due to the excessive single-use plastics and insulated containers used to maintain food temperature. While these services offer undeniable benefits in terms of accessibility and time-saving, their environmental footprint challenges us to weigh short-term convenience against long-term planetary health.

The delivery of physical goods through subscription boxes and e-commerce platforms compounds these concerns. The rise of curated boxes—ranging from clothing to personal care products—has revolutionised retail, enticing consumers with novelty and personalised experiences. However, this model frequently entails frequent shipments with low packing efficiency, leading to inflated transport emissions and excessive waste. For instance, apparel subscriptions may prompt higher consumption rates, increasing demand for fast fashion whose production is notoriously resource-intensive. The environmental consequences ripple upstream to manufacturing, water usage, and landfill burden, highlighting the hidden costs embedded in subscription-driven consumer culture.

Digital media subscriptions, often perceived as low-impact alternatives, also contribute to ecological degradation. Streaming services depend on vast data centres that consume enormous amounts of electricity, often sourced from carbon-intensive grids. The energy footprint of global data traffic rivals that of entire nations, and streaming high-definition video intensifies this demand. Moreover, content platforms frequently refresh libraries, promoting endless consumption patterns that exacerbate resource use. While these services reduce physical waste associated with traditional media formats, their digital energy consumption demands critical scrutiny and innovation towards greener infrastructures.

Confronting the environmental cost of convenience thus requires a multifaceted approach. It begins with heightened consumer awareness—recognising that each subscription, whether digital or physical, implicates broader ecological systems. This awareness motivates more deliberate subscription practices, encouraging choices that prioritise sustainability. For example, consumers might consolidate deliveries to reduce transport emissions or select services with transparent eco-certifications. They may also favour digital consumption with providers committed to renewable energy or participate in circular economy initiatives such as product reuse and recycling programs embedded within subscription models.

Beyond individual action, this inquiry highlights the role of systemic change. It challenges companies to redesign supply chains, invest in sustainable packaging, and innovate energy-efficient data solutions. Subscription providers face mounting pressure to balance profitability with environmental responsibility, as informed consumers increasingly demand transparency and ethical practices. Public policy also plays a crucial role in setting standards and incentivising green innovation within the subscription economy. This collective dimension emphasises that sustainability is not merely a consumer choice but a shared enterprise requiring collaboration across sectors.

Ethical reflection further enriches this conversation by examining how convenience-driven consumption shapes societal values and priorities. The subscription economy's promise of effortless satisfaction can obscure the deeper trade-offs involved, fostering a culture of disposability and instant gratification. By foregrounding environmental costs, this subchapter invites readers to cultivate *mindful consumerism*—an orientation that honours the interconnectedness of financial decisions, ecological integrity, and social wellbeing. Mindfulness encourages resisting the default impulse towards accumulation and instead embracing restraint, intentionality, and responsibility in consumption habits.

Practical tools and strategies conclude this exploration, guiding readers in conducting sustainability audits of their subscriptions. These include assessing the carbon footprint of services, evaluating packaging waste, and investigating corporate sustainability commitments. Readers are equipped with frameworks to recalibrate their subscription portfolios, favouring options that align with ecological values without sacrificing essential needs or quality of life. The aim is not to reject convenience wholesale but to integrate it thoughtfully within a sustainable lifestyle that respects planetary boundaries.

In sum, the environmental cost of convenience is a complex, pressing challenge that demands both individual discernment and systemic transformation. This subchapter offers an authoritative, nuanced perspective that transcends superficial critiques, grounding environmental concerns in the lived realities of subscription culture. It empowers readers to navigate the subscription landscape with informed ethics and practical agency, fostering a future where convenience coexists with ecological stewardship rather than contradiction. Through this deep engagement, budgeting becomes not only an exercise in financial discipline but also a commitment to sustaining the ecosystems that sustain us all.

Mindful Consumerism in a Subscription World

In an age where subscriptions govern much of daily life—from entertainment and education to personal care and even transportation—the question of *what* we consume has become inseparable from the question of *why*. Subscription models, by design, encourage ongoing engagement and habitual spending, often blurring the line between genuine value and compulsive consumption. Against this backdrop, the concept of *mindful consumerism* emerges as a necessary antidote, urging a deliberate alignment between financial choices and one's deepest ethical convictions. This subchapter introduces the framework of *"value-to-values" alignment*—a lens through which readers can audit their subscriptions not only for economic worth but for congruence with personal and collective principles.

At its core, *value-to-values* alignment challenges the prevailing consumerist paradigm that privileges transactional value—the price paid versus the benefit received—over the broader implications of spending decisions. For instance, a streaming service might offer exceptional content and seamless user experience, constituting high transactional value. Yet, if the service perpetuates exploitative labour practices or undermines cultural diversity, the ethical values of many subscribers may be compromised. By shifting focus from *value* alone to include *values*, this framework encourages a holistic evaluation of subscriptions as multidimensional commitments that extend beyond mere convenience or entertainment.

The necessity of such an approach is underscored by the opacity and complexity of modern subscription ecosystems. Consumers rarely possess full visibility into the social, environmental, or political consequences of their spending. Corporate structures, data practices, and supply chains are often obscured behind glossy interfaces and marketing narratives. *Value-to-values* alignment, therefore, demands both critical inquiry and intentionality—tools that empower subscribers to penetrate surface-level appeal and uncover the systemic realities their money supports. This shift moves budgeting from passive maintenance to active ethical engagement.

Real-world applications of this framework abound. Consider the contrasting choices of two readers: one who subscribes to a popular global news outlet but remains unaware of its parent company's political affiliations; another who opts for a smaller, independent publisher whose mission aligns with journalistic integrity and social justice. Both subscriptions offer informational value, yet their *values* differ markedly. Through guided self-assessment, readers can discern which services genuinely resonate with their ethical compass and which might warrant reconsideration or cancellation.

Practical methods for auditing subscriptions form a cornerstone of this subchapter. Readers are introduced to systematic exercises that map current subscriptions against articulated values such as environmental sustainability, social equity, privacy, and cultural preservation. This process involves researching providers' corporate practices, transparency reports, and public controversies, as well as reflecting on how each subscription impacts one's personal sense of integrity. By cultivating this disciplined awareness, consumers can identify misalignments that often go unnoticed in the routine of recurring payments.

Moreover, *value-to-values* alignment confronts the psychological and emotional dimensions of subscription consumption. Loyalty to certain brands or platforms may stem from habit, identity, or perceived necessity rather than genuine ethical endorsement. This framework invites introspection about why certain subscriptions persist despite cognitive dissonance or discomfort with their underlying values. Such reflection fosters a compassionate yet discerning stance—recognising the challenges of disentangling oneself from embedded consumer patterns while affirming the possibility of change.

The conceptual tension between idealism and pragmatism also features prominently in this discussion. Not all consumers have equal access to ethically perfect alternatives; affordability, availability, and convenience remain critical considerations. The *value-to-values* framework acknowledges these constraints and advocates for a graduated, context-sensitive approach that balances aspirational ethics with lived realities. Even incremental shifts toward greater alignment can cumulatively effect meaningful change, both personally and systemically.

This framework resonates with emerging movements in conscious capitalism and ethical finance, situating budgeting within broader currents of social transformation. It challenges the notion of economic participation as morally neutral or detached from identity, emphasising instead that money management is an extension of ethical agency. Readers are encouraged to view their subscription choices not as isolated transactions but as components of a larger ethical narrative—one that shapes culture, politics, and the environment.

Philosophically, the *value-to-values* alignment reframes consumption as a form of storytelling and self-expression. Subscriptions become chapters in a personal and communal story, revealing what individuals stand for and aspire toward. This narrative dimension adds depth to budgeting, transforming it into an ongoing project of coherence and authenticity. Through this lens, financial clarity becomes a vehicle for spiritual and moral clarity.

In conclusion, this subchapter equips readers with both conceptual insight and actionable tools to navigate the subscription landscape with intentionality and integrity. By fostering a mindful consumerism rooted in *value-to-values* alignment, it empowers readers to reclaim control over their recurring expenditures, ensuring that their spending habits serve not only their needs but also their highest ethical commitments. This transformative approach to budgeting promises to reshape the relationship between money, morality, and meaning in a subscription-dominated world.

Capitalism, but Make It Conscious

Capitalism, as the dominant economic system of the modern world, shapes not only markets and production but also the very rhythms of daily life and the contours of personal identity. It offers unprecedented opportunities for innovation, wealth creation, and individual agency, yet it also presents profound challenges, particularly in its capacity to subsume individuals within cycles of consumption, debt, and perpetual growth. The question at the heart of this subchapter is both urgent and nuanced: How can one inhabit capitalism without being consumed by it? This is not a call for wholesale rejection but an invitation to engage capitalism consciously, wielding philosophical tools that transcend mere financial calculations and cultivate a form of economic participation infused with ethical awareness and personal sovereignty.

To understand the complexity of living consciously within capitalism, one must first recognise capitalism's ambivalent character. It is a system propelled by market logic—competition, profit maximisation, and commodification—yet it is also embedded in social relations and cultural meanings. The subscription economy, emblematic of contemporary capitalism, encapsulates this duality by offering convenience and connection while often fostering dependency and alienation. The tension lies in the fact that capitalism's mechanisms are neither inherently good nor evil; their effects depend largely on how individuals and communities relate to them. This insight sets the stage for an inquiry into how to *live with capitalism* rather than be *lived by it.*

Philosophically, this inquiry draws on traditions that emphasise *agency*, *mindfulness*, and *ethical discernment.* Existentialist thinkers like Simone de Beauvoir and Jean-Paul Sartre stress the importance of *authenticity*—the capacity to act deliberately in the face of structural pressures. Similarly, the Stoics advocate for distinguishing between what lies within our control and what does not, focusing energy on conscious choices rather than external forces. These perspectives provide a foundational mindset for navigating capitalism with clarity: recognising systemic constraints while refusing to surrender one's moral and existential autonomy.

A critical tool in this endeavour is the cultivation of *intentionality* in spending and consumption. Beyond budgeting as arithmetic, this approach frames financial decisions as expressions of values and identity. It invites individuals to interrogate why they subscribe to certain services or brands: Is it out of habit, social expectation, or genuine alignment with personal principles? Such reflection transforms spending from passive acquiescence to active authorship, enabling one to design a financial life that supports rather than undermines one's sense of purpose. This shift from reactivity to proactivity is a cornerstone of conscious capitalism.

Conscious capitalism also requires a nuanced understanding of *interdependence.* Capitalism is often critiqued for fostering atomisation and competition, yet it is equally a networked system where actions ripple through economies and ecosystems. Recognising this interconnectedness motivates a broadened ethical horizon—where consumer choices consider not only personal benefit but collective wellbeing. Subscription choices thus become a form of voting with one's wallet, a practice that can either reinforce exploitative practices or nurture sustainable and equitable alternatives.

The practical challenge, however, lies in translating philosophical insights into sustainable habits within an environment designed to prioritise engagement over emancipation. Subscription traps, frictionless renewals, and targeted marketing exploit psychological vulnerabilities and often thwart conscious control. To counteract these tendencies, this subchapter offers strategies that blend philosophical reflection with pragmatic tactics: setting clear financial intentions, establishing mindful consumption rituals, and embracing periodic 'subscription sabbaths' as acts of reclaiming time and agency.

Further, this approach recognises the emotional landscape of capitalist participation. Feelings of shame, envy, or inadequacy often accompany financial decisions, complicating the path to conscious living. Embracing *self-compassion* becomes essential, allowing for mistakes and setbacks without surrendering commitment to ethical engagement. This emotional resilience supports a sustainable practice of mindful capitalism that resists perfectionism and instead cultivates continuous growth and learning.

Contemporary examples illustrate the viability of conscious capitalism in practice. Movements such as community-supported agriculture, ethical fashion cooperatives, and localised renewable energy initiatives demonstrate how economic activity can be reimagined to prioritise human and ecological flourishing over abstract profit. These models offer inspiration and blueprints for embedding consciousness within capitalist participation, challenging the notion that capitalism must be synonymous with exploitation or alienation.

Importantly, this subchapter does not advocate a retreat from the market but a *reclamation* of its potential as a site of creativity and ethical action. It invites readers to view capitalism as a living system—one that is continually shaped by the choices and values of its participants. Through conscious budgeting and subscription management, individuals contribute to this shaping, affirming that capitalism's future is not predetermined but subject to human agency and moral imagination.

In navigating this complex terrain, readers are equipped not only with practical financial tools but with a robust philosophical framework that integrates ethics, psychology, and economics. This integration fosters a form of economic citizenship that is reflective, responsible, and resilient—one capable of withstanding the seductions and pressures of the subscription economy without losing sight of deeper human values.

Ultimately, *Capitalism, but Make It Conscious* is a call to embody a richer relationship with money—one that honours both material realities and spiritual aspirations. It redefines budgeting as an act of empowerment and alignment, positioning conscious capitalism not as a utopian ideal but as a pragmatic, ongoing project of living with intention amid complexity. Through this lens, readers are invited to reclaim their financial lives from automation and apathy, cultivating a presence and purpose that defy the passive consumption patterns that subscription culture often engenders.

Chapter 8
Designing a Living Budget

Budgeting, once imagined as a grid of numbers obediently confined to spreadsheets, must now be re-envisioned to meet the unsettled and shifting demands of contemporary life. It is no longer sufficient to balance rows of figures or calculate neat percentages. Human experience resists such rigidity. Our finances ebb and flow with mood, with the turn of the seasons, with the weight of circumstance. Precision and order remain useful, yes, but they cannot capture the messier truth of living with money. This chapter urges a departure from static systems, inviting a view of budgeting as something alive—breathing, mutable, capable of holding not only income and expense but also value, longing, and psychological weather.

At the heart of this reimagining lies a simple recognition: budgeting is not merely technical, it is creative. It can, in fact, be a kind of care for the self. The idea of a "financial moodboard" conveys this spirit—a collage, both visual and conceptual, that maps the resonance of different financial choices against one's emotional state, stage of life, and aspirations. Like arranging a room or planning a wardrobe, this practice encourages attentiveness and intentionality. The point is not to reduce but to curate, to let money reflect what nourishes rather than what merely numbs. A budget, seen in this light, becomes less an austere cage and more a mirror of inner alignment.

Crucial, too, is an attunement to what might be called the rhythm of enough. Modern consumer culture, turbocharged by subscriptions and endless availability, nudges us into the belief that "more" is the only answer. Yet consumption, if we listen closely, carries its own cadences: there are moments when indulgence feels right, and others when restraint brings relief. To budget well is to learn these cadences, to cultivate discernment in saying yes or saying no. And this rhythm is never static—it evolves with circumstance, with the shifting of priorities, with the quiet recognition that sufficiency can be as satisfying as abundance.

The psychological dimension deepens further when we introduce the notion of flow-state finance. Borrowed from positive psychology, it suggests that financial management can be not only orderly but pleasurable, even energising. Anxiety and guilt often accompany talk of money, yet when budgeting aligns with genuine values and meaningful goals, it can foster confidence, mastery, and a quiet sense of creativity. Here, budgeting is not a burden imposed from without but a structure shaped from within, supporting decisions that feel deliberate rather than dictated.

Among the most practical tools in this living system is what might be called the joy audit. It asks, gently but firmly: which expenses, which subscriptions, bring real satisfaction? And which carry only the weight of obligation, dullness, or guilt? The exercise is not punitive; it does not scold. Instead, it invites pruning with compassion. By trimming away what no longer serves, we create space for what does. A joy audit transforms the budget from a logbook of sacrifice into a celebration of what genuinely matters, fostering both emotional clarity and financial coherence.

The theory here is not left abstract. Scattered through the chapter are stories of individuals and families who have remade their financial practices—sometimes radically, sometimes subtly—to echo their changing values. They show what it looks like to move through seasonal variations with grace, to anchor money decisions in joy rather than dread, to reclaim sovereignty in a subscription-heavy world. Their accounts remind us that a living budget is not only possible but liberating.

This perspective sits within the larger currents of financial mindfulness and ethical consumerism that run throughout this book. But here the conversation advances from principle to practice. The living budget is presented not as an idealised theory but as a workable framework—elastic enough to grow with its keeper, yet grounded enough to offer structure. It is budgeting reimagined as adaptive, responsive, holistic.

To embrace this approach is to accept budgeting as an ongoing dialogue: a conversation between self and circumstance, between aspiration and reality. It honours the layered complexity of financial decision-making in the present age. Moving beyond the rigidity of static spreadsheets, it offers instead a practice that is disciplined yet forgiving, structured yet supple, precise yet capable of joy. Such a budget is not simply a financial plan—it is a companion, evolving as we evolve, urging us toward a more deliberate and flourishing life.

Beyond the Spreadsheet

Budgeting, as conventionally practised, is often reduced to a rigid ledger of figures—a spreadsheet populated by income, expenses, and projections, locked in the cold logic of arithmetic. Yet this traditional method, while precise, overlooks a fundamental truth: money management is not merely a numerical exercise but a deeply human endeavour, intimately tied to the rhythms of daily life, fluctuating emotions, and shifting priorities. To confine budgeting strictly within the limits of columns and formulas is to deny its full potential as a dynamic, adaptive practice. This subchapter urges a reimagining of budgeting beyond spreadsheets, inviting readers to design systems that respond fluidly to mood, season, and context, cultivating financial habits that are both resilient and responsive.

The challenge lies in recognising that financial decisions are rarely made in isolation from the broader texture of life. Seasonal changes bring new needs and desires—holidays prompt gift-giving and travel expenses; summer may increase spending on outdoor activities, while winter could shift priorities toward home heating and cozy comforts. Likewise, emotional states heavily influence consumption patterns. Moments of stress might provoke impulsive purchases, while times of contentment can foster thoughtful, deliberate spending. Any budgeting framework that ignores these human factors risks alienation and failure, as it demands an unnatural rigidity from inherently flexible circumstances.

Central to this evolved approach is the concept of the *financial moodboard*—an innovative, practice-oriented tool designed to capture the qualitative nuances that traditional budgets overlook. Borrowing from the creative arts, a moodboard is a collage of images, words, colours, and symbols that visually and conceptually represent an individual's financial aspirations, challenges, and contexts. Applied to budgeting, this tool helps crystallise the emotional and situational variables influencing spending habits. Rather than merely calculating where money goes, it encourages reflection on why certain expenses matter at particular moments and how they align with evolving personal values.

Creating a financial moodboard involves curating elements that resonate with one's current life stage and aspirations. For example, a young professional might include images representing career advancement, travel, and social engagement, juxtaposed with reminders of saving goals or debt repayment. In contrast, a retiree's moodboard may emphasise health, leisure, and legacy planning. This process externalises internal financial narratives, offering a tangible reference point to guide budgeting decisions that accommodate both numbers and nuances. The moodboard transforms budgeting into an expressive, intentional act—a living artefact that can be revisited and revised as life unfolds.

This fluid method also acknowledges the imperative to break free from the binary thinking that constrains traditional budgeting: the stark opposition of indulgence versus deprivation. Life's complexity demands a more sophisticated calculus, one that honours *the rhythm of enough*—the personal cadence of spending that balances enjoyment with responsibility. Identifying this rhythm requires attunement to personal values and circumstances, recognising when to embrace financial flexibility and when to tighten control. The financial moodboard becomes instrumental here, capturing shifting priorities and emotional currents that inform these decisions.

Psychological insights further deepen this reframing. Drawing on principles from behavioural economics and positive psychology, budgeting can be approached as a practice designed not just to restrict but to energise and align with one's authentic self. The concept of *flow-state finance* posits that when budgeting supports clear goals, reflects meaningful values, and adapts to life's flux, it can generate feelings of agency and satisfaction. This contrasts sharply with the anxiety and resistance often elicited by inflexible financial plans. By integrating emotional intelligence into budgeting systems, individuals are empowered to navigate their financial lives with grace and resilience.

Crucially, this paradigm encourages *mindful pruning*—a reflective process that moves away from guilt-driven austerity towards compassionate curation. Through what might be termed a *joy audit*, readers are prompted to examine their subscriptions and expenses with questions that probe emotional resonance and utility: Which commitments genuinely enhance well-being? Which induce stress or numbness? Which serve habit rather than purpose? This process is not about punishment but presence—learning to disengage from financial obligations that no longer align with lived reality or values.

Real-world applications illustrate the potency of this approach. Consider a family navigating the financial shifts brought on by a child's transition to college. Rather than imposing a static budget, they create a seasonal financial moodboard that acknowledges increased travel, fluctuating living costs, and emotional milestones. This adaptive framework allows them to anticipate expenses and adjust spending with intention, preserving both financial stability and family harmony. Similarly, a freelance professional might use a moodboard to visualise periods of feast and famine, enabling proactive saving strategies that respect income variability.

This expanded conception of budgeting also dialogues with broader themes of financial ethics and sustainability explored elsewhere in the book. By encouraging alignment between spending and evolving values, it fosters a form of economic mindfulness that transcends mere self-interest. The financial moodboard becomes a tool for conscious consumption, facilitating choices that consider personal well-being alongside social and environmental impact.

Ultimately, the invitation is clear: budgeting need not be a static chore imposed by spreadsheets and calculators but a living, evolving conversation with oneself. By embracing mood, seasonality, and context as integral components, readers are equipped to design financial systems that reflect the fullness of human experience. This approach honours the complexity of money management today—complexity not as a source of anxiety but as an opportunity for creativity, presence, and empowerment. Through tools like the financial moodboard and practices attuned to life's rhythms, budgeting transforms from a rigid obligation into a supportive companion on the path toward financial and personal flourishing.

The Rhythm of Enough

The notion of "enough" is deceptively simple yet profoundly complex when applied to personal finance. In a society saturated with messages urging constant acquisition and consumption, defining what constitutes *enough* is not merely a question of numbers or budgets but a deeply personal and dynamic process. This subchapter invites readers to discover their unique *rhythm of enough*—an intuitive cadence that guides when to say yes to spending and when to pause, challenging the pervasive binary framing of financial choices as either deprivation or indulgence. Recognising this rhythm transforms budgeting from a restrictive discipline into a liberating practice, aligning expenditure with authentic needs and values.

At its core, the rhythm of enough confronts a cultural paradox: we are inundated with options and incentives to consume, yet many experience chronic dissatisfaction, often oscillating between guilt over perceived excess and frustration over perceived scarcity. This polarity suggests an underlying failure to calibrate consumption in a way that is sustainable, meaningful, and emotionally healthy. Contemporary behavioural science reveals that humans do not thrive under strict scarcity or overindulgence; instead, psychological well-being flourishes in balance, which is inherently fluid and context-dependent. The rhythm of enough therefore demands an ongoing attunement to both internal states and external circumstances.

Understanding this rhythm requires moving beyond the rigid frameworks of traditional budgeting, which often present financial management as a series of fixed limits or goals. Instead, it encourages embracing variability as an intrinsic aspect of life. Seasonal changes, social obligations, emotional fluctuations, and shifting priorities all influence spending patterns. For example, a creative professional may consciously increase discretionary spending during periods of artistic inspiration or collaboration, while adopting austerity in quieter months. This adaptive approach aligns with research from positive psychology that highlights the benefits of *psychological flexibility*—the capacity to adjust behaviour in response to evolving conditions without losing sight of core values.

A critical step in discovering one's rhythm of enough involves cultivating mindfulness around spending decisions. This means pausing to reflect on the motivations behind each expenditure and the emotions it evokes. Is a purchase an expression of genuine need or aligned joy, or is it a response to stress, social pressure, or habit? These distinctions matter because they shape the sustainability of financial behaviours. Mindfulness practices, widely studied for their efficacy in reducing impulsivity and enhancing self-regulation, offer practical tools to develop this awareness. Through intentional reflection, individuals begin to recognise patterns in their financial life, discerning moments when spending is nourishing and those when restraint is more beneficial.

This nuanced perspective also dismantles the cultural stigma often attached to financial restraint, reframing it not as deprivation but as *deliberate choice*. Resisting a purchase can be an act of empowerment rather than sacrifice. Conversely, mindful indulgence is celebrated as a legitimate and valuable aspect of well-being. This reframing is essential to breaking free from the rigid dichotomy that positions budgeting as either austerity or hedonism. Instead, it cultivates a mindset in which spending is understood as a *rhythmic flow*—a series of intentional decisions calibrated to meet changing needs and desires over time.

Practical examples underscore how individuals and families can operationalise this concept. Consider a household that integrates a "spending pause" ritual each month: a dedicated period during which non-essential purchases are temporarily suspended, allowing space for reflection on what feels genuinely necessary or joyful. This pause is not punitive but regenerative, creating room to recalibrate priorities. Alternatively, some adopt a *spending season* approach, designating certain periods for focused indulgence (such as holidays or celebrations) balanced by seasons of conservation. These strategies demonstrate that budgeting infused with rhythmic awareness supports both financial health and emotional well-being.

Philosophically, the rhythm of enough invites a re-examination of societal narratives around consumption and success. Consumer culture often equates happiness with accumulation, reinforcing a relentless pursuit of "more" that undermines contentment. By contrast, attuning to one's rhythm of enough encourages values-centred living, where financial decisions reflect not external expectations but intrinsic priorities. This shift echoes ethical and existential traditions that emphasise *moderation* and *presence* as pathways to a fulfilled life. It challenges readers to define success not by net worth or material acquisition but by harmony between resources and aspirations.

Moreover, this approach has broader implications for sustainability and social responsibility. When individuals cultivate a personal rhythm of enough, they naturally contribute to reducing overconsumption and its attendant environmental impacts. This alignment of personal finance with ecological awareness amplifies the ethical dimension of budgeting, reinforcing its role as a tool for conscious living. In this way, discovering one's rhythm of enough transcends individual benefit to encompass collective well-being.

In summary, the rhythm of enough is an invitation to move beyond mechanical budgeting towards a richer, more humanised financial practice. It recognises that financial choices are embedded in the lived experience, shaped by moods, seasons, and shifting contexts. By fostering mindfulness, flexibility, and values alignment, this concept empowers readers to navigate spending with clarity and compassion—knowing when to say yes and when to pause, not as an imposed discipline, but as an authentic expression of their financial and emotional lives. This calibrated balance between indulgence and restraint marks a transformative step towards sustainable, joyful financial stewardship.

Flow-State Finance

Budgeting is often dismissed as a dry, mechanical chore—a series of calculations and cutbacks that drains energy rather than fuels it. Yet, what if budgeting could be transformed into a *flow-state experience*, a dynamic practice that aligns with one's values, energises the mind, and nurtures emotional well-being? This subchapter explores how the principles of positive psychology—particularly the concept of flow—can be applied to create a budgeting process that is not only effective but also deeply rewarding and sustainable. By reframing financial management as an intrinsically engaging activity, individuals can break free from the drudgery and anxiety often associated with money and instead cultivate a sense of mastery, purpose, and joy.

The psychological concept of *flow*, first articulated by Mihaly Csikszentmihalyi, describes a state of complete immersion and focused engagement in an activity where challenge and skill are optimally balanced. Flow is characterised by a loss of self-consciousness, a distortion of time, and an intrinsic reward that motivates ongoing participation. While traditionally studied in creative and athletic pursuits, flow is equally applicable to mundane yet essential tasks—including budgeting—when these tasks are designed to engage and inspire rather than frustrate or bore. This shift requires reimagining budgeting not as a list of prohibitions but as an evolving practice that harmonises financial goals with personal growth and emotional fulfilment.

One of the fundamental barriers to entering a flow state in budgeting is the common framing of financial management as reactive and restrictive. When budgets are imposed as rigid, punitive frameworks, they can provoke resistance, guilt, or apathy. Positive psychology encourages a *strengths-based approach* that focuses on what energises and motivates individuals. For budgeting, this means designing systems that are flexible, context-aware, and aligned with personal values. For instance, setting attainable micro-goals, celebrating incremental progress, and incorporating creativity into budget planning can transform a task into an absorbing and satisfying experience. This approach reflects findings from behavioural economics showing that positive reinforcement and autonomy enhance commitment and sustained behaviour change.

To illustrate, consider the example of a young professional who integrates budgeting into their weekly routine as a mindful practice. Instead of treating expense tracking as a chore, they allocate time to review spending in a quiet, distraction-free environment, using visual tools like charts and colour coding that make financial patterns visually compelling. They pair this review with reflective journaling, noting not just numbers but feelings and intentions connected to each expenditure. This ritual transforms budgeting into a form of self-expression and insight, fostering a deeper connection to money that goes beyond balance sheets to encompass identity and purpose.

Such experiential richness mirrors the core elements of flow: clear goals, immediate feedback, and a sense of control.

Another key aspect of flow-state finance is the balance between challenge and skill. A budget that is too simplistic risks boredom, while one that is overly complex invites frustration. Crafting a personalised budgeting framework involves calibrating difficulty—such as setting realistic savings targets or gradually refining spending categories—to maintain engagement without overwhelming the individual. This calibration is dynamic, evolving with changing life circumstances and financial literacy. Apps and digital tools that adapt to user behaviour and offer tailored suggestions exemplify this principle, providing scaffolding that supports skill development and fosters confidence.

Moreover, positive psychology emphasises the importance of *meaning and purpose* in motivating behaviour. Budgets anchored in values and long-term aspirations are more likely to sustain engagement. Integrating a vision for financial wellbeing—such as funding education, travel, or philanthropy—imbues budgeting with significance that transcends immediate constraints. This perspective reframes budgeting as an active, creative project rather than passive limitation. The emotional reward of aligning spending with personal goals enhances motivation and resilience, qualities essential for navigating financial challenges.

The emotional dimension of flow-state finance also includes cultivating *self-compassion* and reducing financial shame. Positive psychology advocates for kindness towards oneself in the face of setbacks, viewing mistakes as opportunities for learning rather than failure. Applying this mindset to budgeting can alleviate the common stress and anxiety linked to money management, replacing it with curiosity and acceptance. Practically, this might involve regular check-ins to assess progress without judgment and adjusting budgets with an understanding of life's unpredictability.

Technological innovations offer new avenues to facilitate flow in budgeting. Interactive platforms incorporating gamification, real-time feedback, and social support tap into intrinsic motivation and community engagement. For example, challenges that reward mindful spending or collaborative savings goals can enhance commitment and enjoyment. However, critical awareness is necessary to avoid manipulation or superficial engagement; tools must empower users rather than exploit behavioural biases.

While flow-state finance promises a more energising and rewarding budgeting experience, it also challenges prevailing norms that treat money as merely transactional or stressful. Embracing this paradigm requires cultural and individual shifts towards viewing financial stewardship as an integral part of holistic wellbeing. It calls for integrating emotional intelligence, self-awareness, and intentionality into everyday money practices—transforming budgeting from a burden into a source of clarity and vitality.

In sum, applying principles from positive psychology to budgeting invites a profound redefinition of financial management. By designing systems that adapt to mood, skills, and values, and by fostering intrinsic motivation and self-compassion, budgeting can become a flow experience—one that not only secures economic stability but also enriches life with meaning, satisfaction, and emotional resonance. This alignment offers a pathway to sustainable financial habits rooted in empowerment rather than obligation, marking a pivotal evolution in how we relate to money in the modern world.

The Joy Audit

In the relentless swirl of subscription services that saturate modern life, a crucial question is often overlooked: which of these monthly charges genuinely enhance our wellbeing, and which quietly erode it? The concept of a *Joy Audit* invites a transformative pause—an intentional, reflective assessment of subscriptions not merely in terms of cost, but in relation to the emotional landscape they create. This audit challenges the transactional mindset that reduces subscriptions to line items on a ledger and instead fosters a nuanced conversation about pleasure, guilt, and presence in our financial lives. By adopting this practice, readers can transcend the binary of austerity versus excess, approaching financial pruning not as punishment, but as a conscious alignment with what truly enriches their lives.

The proliferation of subscription services—streaming platforms, digital learning, meal kits, wellness apps, and more—has led to a paradox of abundance coupled with emotional ambivalence. While the convenience and variety are unparalleled, many find themselves trapped in a cycle of paying for services they rarely use or that fail to deliver satisfaction. Psychological research into consumer behaviour underscores this dissonance: *hedonic adaptation* causes the initial excitement of a new subscription to fade, often replaced by numbness or regret. In this context, the Joy Audit becomes a vital tool for reclaiming agency, enabling individuals to discern which services continue to spark genuine joy and which merely fill a void or soothe anxiety temporarily.

Conducting a Joy Audit requires more than an uncritical review of financial statements; it demands *mindful presence*. This means cultivating an honest, compassionate awareness of how each subscription interacts with one's emotional state and values. For example, a streaming service might provide genuine relaxation and connection during stressful periods, while at other times contributing to procrastination or screen fatigue. Similarly, a wellness app might inspire motivation when engaged mindfully but become a source of guilt when neglected. This duality illustrates why the Joy Audit is not a one-time purge but an ongoing dialogue, sensitive to the ebbs and flows of life's rhythms.

One practical approach to a Joy Audit involves reflective journaling combined with targeted questions designed to probe the affective impact of each subscription. Readers might ask themselves: *When did I last use this service? What feelings did it evoke before, during, and after? Does maintaining this subscription align with my current priorities and values?* By mapping these emotional responses alongside financial data, individuals create a textured narrative of their spending, revealing patterns invisible in traditional budgeting. This practice echoes techniques from *narrative therapy*, which emphasises the power of storytelling to reshape one's relationship with personal challenges—in this case, financial decision-making.

Crucially, the Joy Audit reframes pruning not as a punitive act but as an expression of self-care and intentionality. Rather than viewing subscription cancellations as failures or sacrifices, they become empowered choices to cultivate space—both financial and emotional—for what matters most. This perspective mitigates the common experience of *decision fatigue* and financial guilt, replacing it with clarity and kindness. It also invites an ethical dimension: each subscription retained or discarded is a statement about the values one wishes to embody and support, connecting back to broader themes of conscious consumerism explored throughout this book.

The Joy Audit also reveals cultural and systemic dimensions of subscription engagement. Many subscriptions are designed to exploit psychological vulnerabilities—*fear of missing out (FOMO)*, social comparison, or the desire for convenience—thereby encouraging inertia and overconsumption. A critical component of the Joy Audit involves developing *meta-awareness* of these dynamics, fostering resilience against marketing tactics that masquerade as personal choice. This awareness empowers readers to disentangle authentic joy from manufactured desire, deepening financial literacy beyond numbers into the realm of emotional intelligence.

Consider the case of a mid-career professional who, through a Joy Audit, recognised that her numerous online learning subscriptions—initially intended to bolster her skills—had become sources of stress and self-reproach due to overwhelming content and competing demands. By consciously cancelling the majority and curating a select few aligned with her career goals and learning style, she experienced a reduction in anxiety and a renewed enthusiasm for growth. This example illustrates how pruning with presence not only conserves capital but enhances mental and emotional bandwidth, fostering a healthier relationship with money and self-development.

The Joy Audit process can be supplemented by technological tools designed to increase transparency and control over subscriptions. Apps that aggregate and categorise subscriptions offer quantitative insights, but pairing these with qualitative reflection remains essential to capture the emotional nuance. Furthermore, community forums and peer support can provide encouragement and shared wisdom, reinforcing that subscription pruning is a common challenge rather than an individual failing.

Ultimately, the Joy Audit advocates for a *holistic approach to budgeting*—one that honours the complexity of human experience. It invites readers to recognise that financial wellbeing is inseparable from emotional wellbeing, and that money decisions are deeply embedded in identity, culture, and aspiration. By shifting the focus from guilt-ridden austerity or mindless accumulation to joyful alignment, the Joy Audit offers a sustainable pathway toward financial clarity that nourishes rather than diminishes the self.

This practice is not a panacea but a profound invitation to reclaim financial agency with wisdom and grace. It demands courage to confront uncomfortable truths and curiosity to explore new possibilities. Yet, in doing so, it promises liberation from the shadow of subscription fatigue and the emergence of a budgeting practice suffused with presence, meaning, and joy.

Chapter 9
Teaching Financial Mindfulness to the Next Generation

Childhood and adolescence are unfolding today in a landscape that would have been almost unrecognisable to those who grew up a generation ago. The playground, the classroom, even the living room television—so many of these spaces have migrated into digital form, mediated by subscriptions. Gaming platforms, educational apps, streaming catalogues that never seem to end: for many young people, these are not add-ons but the very fabric of daily life. And yet, while access is seamless, the underlying structures—financial, psychological, cultural—often remain opaque. The subscription has become ubiquitous, and with it comes a new challenge: how to foster financial mindfulness in a generation for whom money is at once everywhere and strangely intangible.

To understand what it means to grow up within this saturated environment is to face questions that are neither simple nor fleeting. Autonomy, value, agency—each takes on new dimensions in a world where ownership is porous and invisible expenses accumulate in the background. Earlier generations handled cash, tallied accounts, felt the weight of money in their hands. Today's digital natives are nudged and steered by algorithms designed not for their wellbeing but for engagement and profit. Being a customer has shifted into something far more entangled, where children and adolescents often find themselves drawn into cycles of quiet, recurring expenditure—habits shaped less by deliberate choice than by the design of the systems around them. The task before us, then, is to rethink financial education so that it keeps pace: no longer the simple piggy bank lesson, but an initiation into digital economics, emotional awareness, and ethical consumption.

Introducing these ideas to the young requires more than reciting definitions. It asks for an approach that speaks their language, acknowledges their digital fluency, and yet broadens it into literacy. Lessons must move from abstraction into lived experience. Instead of treating saving and spending as fixed rules, we can encourage experimentation: digital allowances, carefully framed, create safe laboratories where children can make choices, see outcomes, and learn under guidance. Parents, teachers, mentors—each can use these moments to cultivate habits of reflection, patience, and intentionality. In many ways, these small experiments form the bedrock of financial maturity.

But education should not stop at restraint. To limit financial learning to "don't overspend" is to flatten the imagination. A richer approach nurtures creativity alongside prudence. How might resources be channelled into projects that matter? What experiences outweigh the fleeting rush of yet another subscription? Conversations between adults and children—budgeting together for holidays, weighing wants against longer-term goals—can spark curiosity and resilience. In such exchanges, financial awareness becomes less about restriction and more about shaping a life aligned with one's own values. It is here that young people can begin questioning the norms of their environment, resisting the drift into passive consumption, and practising the art of choosing deliberately.

This chapter goes further, advocating for the raising of "rebels, not renters"—youth who learn to assert autonomy in an economy that often reduces them to perpetual subscribers. Ownership, both tangible and psychological, must be cultivated deliberately. To do so is to challenge the culture of instant gratification that pervades so much of digital life. Patience, self-discipline, ethical reflection—these are not quaint virtues but necessary counterweights. The point is not to tear down capitalism altogether, but to give young people the skills to inhabit it wisely: to see its opportunities clearly while guarding against its more corrosive traps.

Drawing together contemporary research, practical exercises, and vivid examples, this chapter offers a guide for parents, educators, and communities alike. It sketches ways to equip young people with not only financial competence but emotional acuity and ethical grounding. Subscription culture, with all its convenience and peril, is not going away. But we can raise a generation ready to meet it—youth who carry into adulthood not only digital savvy but also a deeper sense of freedom, agency, and responsibility. In the end, the true lesson is larger than money: it is about shaping citizens who can navigate complexity without surrendering their autonomy.

Born Into the Loop

From the moment children today first grasp a tablet or smartphone, they are enveloped in a digital ecosystem defined less by ownership and more by continuous, often invisible, streams of subscriptions. Games that promise endless engagement, learning apps that update in real time, and streaming platforms offering boundless content have become intrinsic to their daily experience. This immersion is not simply a shift in entertainment or education—it constitutes a fundamental transformation in how young people interact with value, choice, and autonomy. Growing up "born into the loop" of subscription culture presents profound implications for their financial literacy, emotional development, and long-term relationship with money.

The subscription model's appeal to children and teenagers lies in its seamless convenience and perpetual novelty. Unlike traditional purchases, subscriptions grant ongoing access without the psychological sting of a single transaction, effectively masking the continuous outflow of money. Platforms such as Roblox, Netflix, or Duolingo have mastered this dynamic, drawing young users into ecosystems that reward engagement and repeat visitation while cultivating habituation. The architecture of these services leverages behavioural science techniques—variable rewards, gamification, and social reinforcement—ensuring that young subscribers not only return frequently but remain emotionally tethered to their subscriptions. The consequence is a shift from episodic consumption to a subscription-dependent mindset, where 'owning' content or services is secondary to constant, often automated, access.

The ramifications extend well beyond the digital interfaces. For parents, educators, and policymakers, this raises challenging questions about agency and control. How can young people develop genuine financial autonomy when their first encounters with money are mediated through near-frictionless, recurring payments they may scarcely comprehend? Unlike physical possessions that can be held, shared, or resold, subscriptions cultivate a relationship defined by access and renewal—concepts that require a more sophisticated cognitive and ethical understanding. The risk is that youth become habituated to a financial environment where spending is divorced from conscious choice, weakening their ability to evaluate value critically or to practice restraint. Long-term, this may foster patterns of passive financial engagement that persist into adulthood, complicating efforts toward sustainable money management.

Yet, growing up amidst subscriptions also offers unique educational opportunities if approached with intentionality. Introducing children to budgeting through digital allowances, where parents allocate limited funds for app subscriptions or in-game purchases, can transform abstract financial concepts into tangible learning moments. Through guided exploration, young people can experience the trade-offs inherent in subscription commitments—the negotiation between instant gratification and deferred benefits, the assessment of quality versus cost, and the development of a personal value system within a commercial ecosystem. These experiences form the bedrock of financial literacy tailored to a subscription-dominant economy.

The cultural dimension of subscription consumption among youth warrants equally critical scrutiny. Subscription services often commodify identity and social belonging, tapping into adolescent desires for community and self-expression. Exclusive access to certain game features, content tiers, or educational resources becomes a marker of status and participation, subtly pressuring young consumers to maintain subscriptions to avoid social exclusion. This intertwining of social capital and financial commitment underscores the emotional stakes of subscription retention and cancellation decisions, complicating straightforward notions of choice. Understanding this social context is essential to fostering resilience and autonomy in young consumers.

Moreover, the environmental and ethical implications of a subscription-saturated youth culture are only beginning to surface. The digital infrastructures supporting subscriptions—data centres, constant device usage, and logistics for physical subscription boxes—contribute to a growing ecological footprint. Educating young people about the broader impact of their consumption habits introduces critical perspectives on sustainability and responsibility, encouraging them to weigh not just personal pleasure but collective consequences.

Ultimately, the phenomenon of children and teens "born into the loop" demands a recalibration of financial education and cultural awareness. It challenges adults to equip younger generations not merely with tools to navigate a subscription economy but with frameworks to critique, resist, and reshape it. By fostering critical thinking, emotional intelligence, and ethical reflection alongside practical skills, we can prepare young people to reclaim agency over their financial futures within an increasingly complex economic landscape. This chapter unpacks these themes in depth, offering nuanced insights and actionable strategies for those invested in guiding the next generation toward mindful, empowered participation in a subscription-driven world.

Digital Allowances, Real Consequences

The financial landscape that children and teenagers navigate today is unlike any previous generation's. From the earliest interactions with digital devices, young people are immersed in ecosystems where spending is often invisible, continuous, and automated. Subscription services for gaming, education, entertainment, and even social engagement dominate their experience, raising urgent questions about how to foster genuine money consciousness in a world where digital transactions are omnipresent yet elusive. The notion of a "digital allowance" emerges as a pivotal framework to introduce budgeting tools and financial literacy in age-appropriate, meaningful ways. This approach not only equips young individuals with practical skills but also cultivates a critical awareness of value, autonomy, and long-term consequences—elements indispensable for responsible financial citizenship in the subscription era.

Introducing budgeting concepts to young people requires careful calibration to developmental stages and cognitive readiness. Conventional financial education, with its emphasis on spreadsheets and numerical precision, often falls short of engaging children or adolescents meaningfully. Instead, the digital allowance system leverages the very medium that shapes their lives—the digital interface—to create experiential learning opportunities. For instance, some parents allocate a monthly or weekly digital currency specifically for app store purchases, in-game upgrades, or streaming subscriptions. This controlled exposure serves as a microcosm of real-world spending, providing tangible feedback loops that are immediate and relatable. It empowers young people to make choices, experience trade-offs, and learn accountability in a safe environment.

Case studies illustrate the transformative potential of digital allowances when combined with guided reflection and dialogue. One notable example is a family who introduced a structured digital budget for their teenage children, allowing a set amount for mobile games and online content subscriptions. Beyond tracking expenditures, the parents engaged their children in regular conversations about why certain purchases felt valuable or regrettable, linking these experiences to broader discussions about desire, impulse, and budgeting priorities. Over time, the children developed an intuitive sense of evaluating cost against enjoyment, shifting from reactive spending to intentional decision-making. This reflects the core objective of financial education: cultivating mindful engagement rather than mere transactional competence.

However, the implementation of digital allowances is not without challenges. The ubiquity of free-to-play models and "freemium" services complicates the clarity of value exchange, as initial access may be free but subsequent progression or enhanced experiences require repeated spending. This structure can obscure the real cost and encourage impulsivity. To counter this, educators and parents must emphasise transparency and boundary-setting, teaching young users to recognise when "free" is a veneer for continuous microtransactions. Tools such as spending caps, time-limited access, and collective budgeting goals can help embed discipline while maintaining autonomy.

Moreover, digital allowances offer a crucial platform to discuss the ethical dimensions of consumption. By examining who benefits from subscription models—platform owners, advertisers, data miners—and at what cost to privacy and agency, young people can cultivate a critical lens toward the digital economy. This awareness is particularly important in subscription environments where behavioural data shapes personalised recommendations and nudges, effectively guiding spending decisions. Introducing concepts of data ethics and consent alongside budgeting tools fosters a holistic financial literacy that encompasses not only dollars and cents but also digital rights and self-determination.

As children mature into adolescents, the frameworks for financial education must evolve to accommodate increasing complexity and social dynamics. Peer influence, identity formation, and emerging independence shape consumption patterns, necessitating nuanced approaches that respect autonomy while offering scaffolding. Interactive budgeting apps designed for teenagers, which incorporate gamified challenges, social accountability features, and educational modules, exemplify innovations aligned with these developmental needs. Such tools encourage users to set personal goals, reflect on spending habits, and receive feedback in engaging formats, blending technology with pedagogy.

Critically, fostering money consciousness through digital allowances and associated practices cannot be a solitary endeavour. Schools, communities, and policymakers have roles to play in creating ecosystems supportive of financial literacy. Curricula that integrate practical budgeting with critical media literacy prepare young people to navigate subscription cultures with discernment. Public initiatives that promote transparency in subscription pricing and consent mechanisms contribute to healthier digital environments. The collaboration between families and institutions strengthens the scaffolding that young consumers need to emerge as financially savvy adults.

Ultimately, introducing budgeting and money consciousness to young people via digital allowances is a proactive response to the realities of contemporary consumption. It moves beyond didactic instruction to experiential learning, grounding abstract financial principles in lived experience. This approach nurtures not only competence but also confidence, agency, and ethical awareness—qualities indispensable for flourishing in a subscription-saturated world. By weaving together practical frameworks, developmental insights, and cultural critique, this subchapter equips readers with the knowledge and tools to guide the next generation toward financial mindfulness and resilience.

Financial Imagination

Amid the relentless tide of consumerism shaping today's youth, fostering *financial imagination* emerges not merely as a strategy but as an imperative. Digital natives, immersed in ecosystems saturated with subscription models, instant gratification, and algorithmically curated desires, face unprecedented challenges in discerning creative autonomy from compulsive consumption. Cultivating financial imagination is about nurturing an active relationship with money—one that privileges *creation, experimentation,* and *agency* over passive spending. This approach invites parents, educators, and mentors to reconceive financial education as a collaborative, imaginative endeavour, where conversations and activities serve as catalysts for deeper reflection and conscious choice. It is a call to reclaim space for imagination in the financial lives of young people, empowering them to envision and enact alternatives to the default consumer logic that dominates their environment.

The digital landscape that envelops today's youth is characterised by rapid-fire access to goods, services, and experiences, often bundled in low-friction subscription packages. While this ecosystem promises convenience and variety, it can also obscure the connection between money, values, and creativity. Financial imagination intervenes here, emphasising *the power to repurpose resources*, to see spending as a means to an expressive end rather than an end in itself. For example, rather than defaulting to subscribing endlessly to entertainment platforms, a financially imaginative young person might allocate resources toward learning creative skills, funding collaborative projects, or investing in physical experiences that foster growth and connection. This pivot from consumption to creation reorients the relationship with money from a cycle of acquisition to one of meaning-making.

Research in developmental psychology and education supports the critical role of imaginative play and creativity in cultivating cognitive and emotional resilience. Extending these insights to financial literacy, it becomes clear that engaging young people's imagination about money facilitates *critical thinking*, *self-efficacy*, and *ethical reflection.*

Instead of treating budgeting and spending as rigid rules, a financially imaginative approach encourages fluidity and adaptability, inviting youth to ask: What possibilities emerge if I reallocate this expense? How might I use my financial resources to build rather than simply consume? These questions open space for a richer dialogue that honours individuality and promotes intentionality.

Practical application of financial imagination involves embedding creative exercises and conversations into everyday learning. Parent-child activities designed around imagining alternative futures or re-envisioning current spending patterns serve as powerful tools. One such exercise might involve creating a 'financial vision board' together, where images and words represent both immediate joys and long-term aspirations linked to money. This visualisation process fosters dialogue about priorities, hopes, and values, allowing children to externalise and refine their financial goals in an accessible, engaging way. Another activity encourages co-creating stories about hypothetical scenarios: How would you spend if you could start fresh? What does your ideal financial life look like, and how do your current habits align with that vision?

Crucially, these imaginative explorations must be rooted in *presence* and *empathy*, avoiding the pitfalls of didacticism or pressure. Conversations framed as open-ended inquiries rather than directives invite young people to articulate their feelings about money without fear of judgement. For instance, a parent might ask, "What did it feel like when you decided to subscribe to that app? What made it exciting or challenging?" Such reflective questioning helps surface emotional undercurrents—such as desire for belonging, boredom, or security—that often drive spending behaviours. Recognising these motivations cultivates emotional intelligence alongside financial savvy, strengthening the young person's capacity for mindful decision-making.

The tension between fostering financial imagination and navigating real-world constraints must also be addressed candidly. Not every young person has the same degree of financial autonomy or access to resources that support creative exploration. Economic precarity, cultural expectations, and systemic inequities shape the parameters within which imagination can flourish. Thus, promoting financial imagination involves advocating for structural support—such as equitable access to educational tools, community programs, and transparent financial products—that enable young people from diverse backgrounds to engage meaningfully with their economic realities. This layered understanding prevents imagination from becoming a privilege of the few and situates it as a collective responsibility.

Examining case studies further illuminates how financial imagination manifests in practice. Consider initiatives where schools integrate project-based budgeting tasks that challenge students to design community improvement plans or social enterprises within fixed budgets. These activities bridge creativity and fiscal discipline, illustrating the dynamic interplay between dreaming and doing. Similarly, programmes that encourage youth to document and reflect on their spending patterns through multimedia storytelling foster both technical skills and narrative agency. These examples underscore that financial imagination thrives where *structure meets freedom*, providing frameworks that both guide and inspire.

Philosophically, fostering financial imagination aligns with broader ethical imperatives to cultivate autonomy and critical consciousness in an age defined by pervasive commodification. It challenges dominant economic narratives that reduce human worth to purchasing power and shifts focus toward *values-driven* and *purposeful* financial engagement. Encouraging youth to imagine alternative financial futures is a radical act of empowerment that resists passive absorption into consumer culture. It equips the next generation not only to survive within capitalism's confines but to actively *reshape* their economic environments in ways that reflect collective well-being.

The pedagogical shift towards financial imagination invites adults to model openness, curiosity, and creative risk-taking with money. This modelling is vital because young people often internalise adult attitudes toward finance as part of their own belief systems. When caregivers approach money with rigidity, anxiety, or resignation, they inadvertently transmit these affective patterns. Conversely, demonstrating flexibility, joy, and thoughtful experimentation with financial choices fosters a fertile ground for children and teens to develop their own imaginative capacities.

In sum, financial imagination offers a transformative lens for rethinking how young people learn about and relate to money. It moves beyond traditional metrics of budgeting and saving to embrace *imaginative engagement*, *ethical reflection*, and *expressive potential.* By embedding creative practices, meaningful dialogue, and structural awareness into financial education, we cultivate a generation capable of navigating the complexities of the subscription economy with agency, resilience, and vision. This reimagining is not merely desirable but necessary to counterbalance the consumerist impulses that dominate digital native experiences. Through financial imagination, we unlock the possibility that young people can become architects of their financial lives, crafting futures rich in choice, creativity, and conscious intention.

Raising Rebels, Not Renters

The subscription economy presents an alluring convenience, offering instant access to entertainment, education, and services for a predictable monthly fee. Yet beneath this surface lies a subtle erosion of autonomy—a steady shift from ownership to renting, from choice to obligation, and from independence to dependency. For younger generations raised amid this subscription saturation, the risk is profound: they may become perpetual renters of their own lives, caught in cycles of consumption that displace genuine agency and delayed gratification. This subchapter confronts this modern predicament head-on, advocating instead for the cultivation of *rebellious financial values*—a spirited embrace of autonomy, ownership, and the discipline to defer gratification as antidotes to the pervasive allure of subscription models. Raising rebels, not renters, becomes a clarion call for parents, educators, and mentors who seek to empower youth to navigate the complexities of contemporary financial life with discernment and integrity.

At its core, the subscription model promises flexibility but frequently delivers entrapment. The psychology of recurring payments exploits behavioural tendencies—such as inertia and the sunk cost fallacy—to bind consumers into ongoing financial commitments that often outlast their actual value or desire for the service. For children and teens growing up in this landscape, the normalization of rental rather than ownership is more than an economic shift; it is a cultural one. It shapes their understanding of what it means to have control over resources, to possess, and to cultivate patience. In cultivating rebels, the goal is to counteract these forces by instilling early and consistent values that celebrate *autonomy over passivity*, *ownership over fleeting access*, and *delayed gratification over instant consumption.*

Autonomy, in this context, is more than financial independence—it is the capacity to make choices aligned with one's deeper values and long-term well-being rather than reactive impulses or marketing-driven persuasion. Teaching young people to recognise and resist the subtle manipulations embedded in subscription contracts fosters critical consciousness. This might involve demystifying auto-renewal clauses, decoding fine print, or exploring the psychological hooks embedded in "free" trials and loyalty rewards. The emphasis is on cultivating *financial literacy as empowerment*, encouraging youth to approach spending as a deliberate act rather than passive acquiescence. When autonomy is embraced, young people learn to question not only what they spend on, but why—and, importantly, what they are sacrificing in exchange.

Delayed gratification is a foundational concept with deep roots in developmental psychology, famously exemplified by the Stanford marshmallow experiment, which linked the ability to wait for a larger reward with long-term success and well-being. In a world of subscription-driven immediacy, however, delayed gratification risks being eclipsed by constant digital temptations and the normalized expectation of instant access. Reclaiming this virtue requires intentional education and modelling. Parents and educators can create structured opportunities for children to save for meaningful goals, encouraging a mindset where financial decisions are tied to *purpose* rather than fleeting pleasure. This nurtures patience and perseverance—qualities that not only support healthier financial habits but also enrich character development and resilience.

Ownership, as a principle, represents a deliberate counterweight to the rental culture. Ownership fosters a sense of responsibility, care, and long-term investment. For young people, this might mean cultivating an appreciation for the value of physical goods—books, musical instruments, bicycles—or even investments in knowledge and skills that cannot be rented but must be earned and maintained. Teaching ownership challenges the disposability that subscription models tacitly encourage. It invites reflection on the lifecycle of possessions and the environmental and psychological costs of ephemeral consumption. Moreover, ownership anchors identity and self-efficacy; it is a form of tangible agency in a world increasingly mediated by abstract digital contracts.

Practical strategies to raise rebels rather than renters are manifold and benefit from integration into everyday life. One approach is *intentional budgeting exercises* that foreground choice and consequence, helping young people differentiate between wants and needs in the context of ongoing subscriptions. Encouraging them to audit their subscriptions periodically fosters mindfulness and accountability. Moreover, involving youth in financial decisions—such as negotiating which services to keep or cancel—promotes critical thinking and empowerment. Case studies abound where families have successfully reduced their digital footprint and subscription expenses by fostering open dialogue and shared decision-making, illustrating that rebellion need not imply deprivation but rather conscious liberation.

The cultivation of these values also invites a reimagining of the cultural narratives surrounding success and consumption. Against dominant narratives equating value with accumulation and instant access, raising rebels requires advocating alternative visions centred on *sufficiency*, *intentionality*, and *community*. Philosophical frameworks—from Stoicism's emphasis on self-control to contemporary calls for slow living—offer rich terrain for embedding these values in practical, age-appropriate ways. Such perspectives help young people understand that true wealth extends beyond material possession to include freedom, agency, and meaningful connection.

Critically, raising rebels demands acknowledging the systemic pressures that perpetuate subscription dependency. The ubiquity of digital platforms, the sophistication of behavioural design, and economic precarity all conspire to constrain choice. Therefore, cultivating autonomy, delayed gratification, and ownership is not solely an individual endeavour but a collective challenge requiring supportive policies, educational reform, and culturally embedded resistance to consumerist excess. By equipping the next generation with tools to navigate and critique these systems, we lay groundwork for a society that values autonomy and sustainability over passive rental.

In synthesising these insights, the imperative to raise rebels rather than renters crystallises as both a practical and ethical project. It calls for a pedagogy of *empowerment*, where young people are guided not just in managing money but in cultivating a stance of active resistance to economic structures that erode agency. This pedagogical shift honours the complexity of growing up in a subscription-saturated world while offering hopeful pathways toward autonomy and authentic ownership. As parents, educators, and mentors embrace this mission, they contribute to a profound cultural renewal—one where financial freedom becomes a lived reality, not an elusive ideal.

Chapter 10
Radical Clarity

Clarity, contrary to popular imagination, is rarely a thunderbolt of sudden revelation. It is, instead, a discipline of remembering—an active, almost stubborn decision to hold fast to what matters most amid the blizzard of noise, novelty, and the small daily forgettings that tug at our focus. As the financial world spins itself into ever more intricate webs of subscription models and automatic renewals, the work required of us is not simply arithmetic. It is radical clarity: a deliberate reclamation of attention, of values, of authorship over one's own life. When approached in this way, budgeting ceases to be a dull administrative chore and takes on the weight of a spiritual practice—an act of sovereignty and identity. This chapter asks the reader to step into that shift, to approach money not as a detached bystander but as the writer of their own story, supported by rituals and reflections capable of sustaining clarity in the long run.

At the core of this reorientation lies the practice of remembering. Subscription culture thrives on invisibility, on charges that slip unnoticed through bank statements, on the ease of disengagement. Clarity stands in sharp opposition to this drift. By returning, month after month, to a structured ritual of review—a "clarity ritual", if you will—one cultivates not just accountability but intimacy with one's financial life. This is not bookkeeping in its narrow sense. It is the mindful pause, the deliberate breath, a chance to measure decisions against the compass of values. In a climate where unconscious spending creeps in almost imperceptibly, such rituals anchor us, ensuring we do not lose ourselves in the tide. They act, quite literally, as a compass—not for numbers alone, but for orienting one's whole life toward what is chosen with intention.

When seen through this lens, budgeting reveals dimensions far beyond the ledger. Money is always telling stories. It speaks of our desires, our fears, our identity-in-progress. To take control of a budget, then, is to reclaim authorship of those stories. It is to acknowledge that every financial decision echoes into the shape of the self. Instead of a language of guilt and scarcity, this reframing opens space for compassion, coherence, and growth. Budgets become less a cage and more a declaration—an articulation of what matters and how resources will be bent to serve it. In short, budgeting becomes identity work.

It is within this framework that the concept of the *Subscription Sabbath* arrives, stark and bracing. Imagine thirty days without the quiet hum of auto-renewals, without the familiar crutch of digital comforts on demand. The Sabbath is not a denial for its own sake but an experiment in freedom. Structured with reflective prompts and journals, the exercise allows participants to observe, with surprising clarity, how much of their life has been mediated by habitual spending. The revelations are rarely confined to finances alone: shifts in attention, in mood, even in the felt sense of sovereignty, begin to surface. To step away from the automatic is to rediscover what truly enriches. And far from punitive, this sabbatical offers empowerment—a chance to reset, to encounter the self unbuffered by the endless churn of subscription culture.

The vision, however, stretches further than a month-long experiment. It speaks to the larger struggle of our time: how to remain whole in an environment designed to scatter our attention and dull our agency. Radical clarity is nothing less than a strategy of reclamation. It suggests that budgeting—so often relegated to the background—may serve as a frontline practice for safeguarding life's most precious currencies: time, focus, and intention. To live passively in such an era is to surrender. To practise remembrance is to design the future, one conscious act at a time.

This chapter, then, is not a sermon on austerity, nor a plea for rigid control. Its purpose is subtler: to offer a weave of philosophical reflection, concrete frameworks, and lived examples that recast budgeting as a dynamic, sustaining practice of clarity. The aim is not denial but discernment; not control but coherence. By cultivating radical clarity, readers arm themselves to navigate complexity with steadiness, presence, and conviction. What begins as the management of money may, in the end, feel like something altogether greater: the recovery of freedom.

And so this opening sets the tone for what follows. It is both an ending and a beginning—a culmination of earlier themes and the threshold of deeper ones. Each subsequent page is a step in the same direction: towards a life where financial decisions are not the residue of distraction but deliberate acts of authorship, carried out with the courage and clarity that such a life demands.

The Practice of Remembering

Clarity in financial life is seldom an accidental discovery; it is the product of a disciplined practice, a conscious act of remembering amid the distractions and complexities that characterise modern living. Every day, individuals navigate a barrage of automated payments, digital subscriptions, and economic choices that threaten to obscure their core values and intentions. The practice of remembering is thus a form of resistance against this erasure—a deliberate effort to retrieve and reaffirm what truly matters in the intricate relationship between money, identity, and purpose. To sustain this clarity requires more than sporadic reflection; it calls for a structured, ongoing ritual designed to reconnect individuals with their financial narratives and priorities.

This article explores the nature of that practice, inviting readers to reconceive clarity not as a static goal but as a dynamic, recurring engagement. At its core lies the recognition that forgetting is a natural cognitive tendency—particularly potent in the domain of finances where out-of-sight, out-of-mind payments accumulate silently, eroding awareness and agency. This is why a *monthly clarity ritual* is indispensable. It provides a disciplined cadence to the act of remembering, a framework that transforms financial review from a tedious obligation into a meaningful act of self-knowledge and empowerment. By periodically stepping back to assess spending through the lens of personal values and long-term goals, individuals reclaim control over their financial destinies.

The ritual itself is multifaceted, incorporating practical financial audits alongside reflective questions that probe deeper emotional and psychological layers. Beyond tallying expenses or calculating budgets, it asks: *Which expenditures align with my values? Where am I investing not just money, but time and attention? What patterns of avoidance or indulgence emerge?* This dual inquiry bridges the quantitative and qualitative aspects of money management, cultivating a holistic awareness that sharpens decision-making. The ritual thereby becomes a mirror reflecting not only financial health but the evolving story of selfhood—a narrative that budgeting alone cannot capture unless consciously attended to.

Real-world applications of such reflective practice reveal its transformative potential. Consider the case of individuals who, through consistent clarity rituals, uncover dormant subscriptions that no longer serve them—services once valued but now habitual drains on resources and attention. More importantly, they begin to recognise how certain spending habits correlate with emotional states such as stress or boredom, enabling targeted behavioural shifts rather than blind cuts. This nuanced approach resists the simplistic dichotomy of deprivation versus indulgence, encouraging an intentional, compassionate stance towards money that honours complexity rather than suppresses it.

Critical reflection on the cultural and technological forces that exacerbate forgetfulness also sharpens the urgency of the practice. The design of many financial systems and platforms subtly encourages disengagement through frictionless spending and obfuscated cancellation processes. Without a committed practice of remembering, individuals risk becoming passive participants in cycles of unconscious consumption. Thus, the ritual serves as a safeguard against the economic and psychological consequences of such design, restoring sovereignty over both attention and capital.

Philosophically, the practice of remembering echoes traditions that link memory with identity and freedom. To remember is to assert continuity and coherence in one's life narrative. When applied to financial mindfulness, this insight challenges prevailing notions of budgeting as mere technical skill, repositioning it as an act of ethical and existential significance. It demands that individuals approach money as an extension of self, intertwined with values and aspirations, rather than a mechanical ledger to be balanced.

The monthly clarity ritual also encourages a temporal perspective that mitigates the anxiety of financial uncertainty. By ritualising reflection, individuals create a rhythm that normalises engagement with money—transforming it from a source of intermittent panic into a regular dialogue. This rhythm fosters resilience, allowing for course corrections that are responsive rather than reactive, informed by both data and introspection.

Moreover, the ritual cultivates a language of financial mindfulness that facilitates communication with others—partners, family members, financial advisors—enhancing transparency and shared understanding. It becomes a tool not only for personal clarity but for relational coherence, supporting healthier dynamics around money that transcend secrecy or conflict.

This article advances practical guidance on how to establish and sustain such a ritual. It outlines methods for integrating financial data review with contemplative journaling and value clarification exercises. These elements work synergistically to deepen insight and foster behavioural change. Readers are invited to customise the ritual according to their own rhythms and contexts, ensuring it remains accessible and impactful rather than burdensome.

In essence, clarity as a practice of remembering is an invitation to reclaim agency in a landscape that increasingly favours automation and disengagement. It foregrounds presence and intentionality as antidotes to forgetfulness and financial drift. This is budgeting elevated to a mindful discipline—a powerful, ongoing commitment to live deliberately in relation to money, thereby securing not just fiscal health but personal sovereignty and meaning.

Every paragraph of this exploration aims to illuminate why and how clarity must be actively cultivated. It offers readers a substantive, nuanced framework to sustain progress beyond transient motivation, empowering them to transform their financial lives through conscious remembrance. The practice of remembering is not a once-off event; it is a vital, cyclical act that safeguards the very essence of what it means to live a purposeful, financially mindful life.

Budgeting as Identity Work

Budgeting is often framed as a purely technical task—a matter of numbers, spreadsheets, and rigid discipline. Yet beneath these surface calculations lies a far richer, more nuanced process: budgeting as identity work. This perspective invites us to see our financial habits not just as external behaviours but as deeply intertwined with who we are, the stories we tell ourselves, and the values we hold dear. When approached as a form of emotional and spiritual alignment, budgeting transcends mere accounting; it becomes an act of reclaiming authorship over our lives, a deliberate shaping of our financial narratives that echoes our evolving selves.

Every person's relationship with money is a narrative in motion, shaped by childhood experiences, cultural messages, and personal triumphs or setbacks. These narratives influence how individuals perceive worth, security, freedom, and success. As readers engage with budgeting beyond its mechanics, they are encouraged to interrogate these inherited or internalised money stories. Are their spending patterns reflective of authentic priorities, or are they repetitions of anxiety, scarcity, or external expectations? Recognising this distinction is the first step toward transformation: the transition from unconscious patterns to conscious authorship.

Reclaiming authorship in budgeting is a process of rewriting these narratives with intention and compassion. It requires embracing financial decisions as expressions of identity rather than mere transactional acts. For example, choosing to prioritise spending on education or creative pursuits can become a statement of personal values and aspirations. Conversely, acknowledging and releasing guilt-laden expenditures may signal a shift toward self-forgiveness and growth. This reframing situates budgeting as a dynamic dialogue between past and future selves, where each choice contributes to an ongoing story of becoming.

Contemporary research in behavioural economics and psychology supports this holistic view. Studies reveal that when individuals perceive budgeting as aligned with their sense of self and purpose, they are more likely to sustain healthy financial behaviours over time. This alignment mitigates the alienation often experienced when budgets feel restrictive or punitive. Instead, budgeting becomes a source of empowerment, a tool for crafting a life congruent with deeply held ethical and emotional truths.

Consider the case of a professional who once equated financial success with conspicuous consumption but gradually redefined success in terms of meaningful relationships and creative freedom. Through reflective budgeting practices, they began allocating resources toward travel, community engagement, and personal development rather than status symbols. This shift did not merely improve their financial health but fostered a profound sense of integrity and coherence between their values and actions.

The spiritual dimension of budgeting emerges in this alignment. Money, far from a neutral resource, acts as an energetic vehicle for manifesting intentions and cultivating gratitude. By approaching budgeting with mindfulness and presence, individuals may discover a sense of sacredness in everyday transactions—a reminder that every dollar spent is a vote for a particular life vision. This sacred perspective dissolves the dichotomy between material and spiritual concerns, inviting a unified approach to wellbeing.

However, embracing budgeting as identity work does not imply a simplistic or idealised narrative. Financial realities often impose constraints that test alignment with values. The challenge lies in navigating these tensions with honesty and creativity, adapting one's money story without surrendering core principles. This may involve difficult trade-offs, strategic sacrifices, or incremental progress. The key is sustaining a reflective stance that honours complexity rather than succumbing to binary thinking.

Practical frameworks for this approach include journaling exercises that prompt examination of the emotional context surrounding spending decisions. Questions such as "What story am I telling myself about this purchase?" or "How does this expenditure reflect who I want to be?" cultivate self-awareness and intentionality. Visual tools like financial moodboards can externalise aspirations and fears, making abstract values tangible and actionable within budgeting decisions.

Furthermore, the social dimension of identity work in budgeting warrants attention. Money stories are often co-constructed within families, communities, and cultural milieus. Engaging others in transparent conversations about values and finances can foster mutual understanding and collective alignment. This relational aspect challenges the isolating stigma sometimes attached to financial discussions and supports a culture of shared empowerment.

Critically, recognising budgeting as identity work invites ethical reflection on the broader economic systems that shape individual choices. It foregrounds questions about how consumer culture, subscription economies, and credit infrastructures influence money stories and constrain autonomy. Readers are encouraged to situate their personal narratives within these larger contexts, discerning how structural forces intersect with inner alignment.

This conceptualisation also challenges the traditional deficit model of budgeting that focuses solely on limitation and control. Instead, it frames budgeting as a creative act, an opportunity for self-expression and values-driven living. This shift resonates with contemporary movements in financial therapy and coaching that integrate emotional intelligence, narrative psychology, and spirituality into money management.

The implications for sustained financial wellbeing are significant. When budgeting is no longer a chore but a meaningful practice of identity affirmation, individuals cultivate resilience and adaptability. They are equipped not only to manage resources effectively but to navigate life's uncertainties with confidence grounded in self-knowledge.

In sum, approaching budgeting as identity work demands a reorientation from mechanical precision to heartfelt engagement. It invites readers to become authors of their financial stories, weaving together numbers and narratives, pragmatism and purpose. This synthesis enriches budgeting with emotional and spiritual depth, transforming it into a vital practice for living authentically and intentionally in a complex economic landscape.

The Subscription Sabbath

Subscription services have become ubiquitous, seamlessly woven into the fabric of daily life—streaming entertainment, digital news, software, fitness apps, meal kits, and more. The convenience is undeniable, yet beneath the surface lies a subtle erosion of autonomy, financial clarity, and intentional living. The "Subscription Sabbath" proposes a radical, deliberate pause: a 30-day suspension from all auto-renewing services to reclaim control, cultivate awareness, and reassess what truly adds value. This practice is more than a financial detox; it is an invitation to interrogate our dependence on subscriptions, to reflect on consumption patterns, and to restore sovereignty over time, attention, and money.

The rationale behind a Subscription Sabbath draws from behavioural economics and psychological research demonstrating how auto-renewals exploit inertia and reduce consumer agency. When payments recur invisibly and consumption is frictionless, individuals often lose sight of the cumulative costs—monetary, cognitive, and emotional. This invisibility fuels a cycle of passive spending where subscriptions accumulate unchecked, sometimes delivering diminishing returns or fostering guilt and numbness rather than joy. A conscious break disrupts this cycle, bringing expenditures into focus and enabling recalibration.

Real-world evidence underscores the transformative potential of such intentional interruptions. Anecdotal reports and emerging studies suggest that individuals undertaking subscription pauses often experience heightened clarity about their true preferences and needs. Many discover that the perceived indispensability of certain services was overstated, while others identify neglected subscriptions worthy of renewal. Crucially, this process empowers individuals to make deliberate choices free from marketing pressure or habitual renewal.

Implementing a Subscription Sabbath requires more than cancelling services; it demands a structured framework that supports reflection, learning, and sustainable change. Journaling and reflection become essential tools in this process, helping to externalise thoughts and emotions about consumption. A curated set of prompts can guide participants to examine questions such as: What emotions arise in the absence of these services? Which subscriptions did I miss, and why? What values and priorities have shifted during this pause? How can I re-engage with services in a way that aligns with my goals and wellbeing?

A thoughtfully designed monthly clarity ritual can accompany the Subscription Sabbath, transforming it from a one-off experiment into an ongoing practice. This ritual might involve reviewing subscription statements, evaluating alignment with current values, and setting intentions for mindful renewal or permanent cancellation. By institutionalising such moments of financial mindfulness, individuals can resist the stealthy creep of unnecessary expenses and cultivate a budget that reflects their evolving identity.

Ethical considerations permeate this practice as well. The Subscription Sabbath invites critical engagement with the broader subscription economy, questioning the sustainability of models predicated on recurring charges and psychological hooks. It also challenges cultural narratives that equate consumption with happiness and self-worth. Through this lens, the Sabbath is an act of resistance—a reclaiming of agency against economic structures designed to commodify attention and foster dependency.

There are practical challenges, of course. For some, certain subscriptions underpin essential services or professional tools, making a complete pause impractical. The Subscription Sabbath can be adapted to individual contexts, encouraging partial sabbaths or staggered breaks that respect necessity while promoting reflection. Moreover, the discomfort of withdrawal or boredom during the pause can surface underlying dependencies, offering fertile ground for growth if approached with curiosity and self-compassion.

From a societal perspective, widespread adoption of subscription sabbaths could signal a shift toward more conscious consumption, prompting service providers to rethink value delivery and customer engagement. It also contributes to financial literacy by normalising active budget management rather than passive acceptance of recurring charges. This cultural shift aligns with broader movements advocating for digital wellbeing, minimalism, and sustainable economics.

Ultimately, the Subscription Sabbath reframes budgeting from a mechanical exercise into a profound dialogue with self and society. It invites readers to step out of autopilot, to rediscover what their money really supports, and to author their financial lives with intention and clarity. Through structured pause and reflection, the act of unsubscribing becomes a gateway to deeper understanding, alignment, and freedom.

The Future is Not Passive

In an age defined by relentless consumption and digital distraction, the future of budgeting demands a radical shift—not merely in how we manage money, but in how we reclaim the very essence of our lives: time, attention, and sovereignty. The conventional view of budgeting as a passive, mechanical task falls short in addressing the complexities of today's economic and psychological landscape. Instead, budgeting must be embraced as an active, conscious practice that confronts the systemic forces eroding our capacity to remember who we are and what truly matters. This chapter closes with a visionary perspective: *budgeting for the age of forgetting is ultimately about remembering*—reclaiming identity, purpose, and autonomy amid the noise.

The challenge we face is multifaceted. Modern life is characterised by an overwhelming abundance of choice, subscription traps that quietly siphon resources, and an ever-accelerating pace that fragments attention. These factors conspire to make budgeting feel like a chore, a series of numbers disconnected from lived experience. Yet this very disconnection obscures the power budgeting holds as a tool for intentional living. When budgetary decisions are reduced to rote arithmetic, the deeper work of aligning spending with values, priorities, and self-understanding is lost. This loss is a form of forgetting—not merely financial amnesia but a broader cultural and existential lapse.

At its core, the future of budgeting as envisioned here is a reclaiming of agency. It insists on budgeting as an act of self-definition, a way to steward not only financial capital but the most precious and finite resources: our time and attention. These are the currencies through which meaning is created. When time and attention are ceded to automated renewals, endless scrolling, or mindless consumption, the individual's capacity to deliberate, reflect, and choose is diminished. Budgeting, then, becomes a practice of reclaiming these capacities—a deliberate act of saying yes to what enriches life and no to what erodes it.

Consider the analogy of memory as a foundation for identity. Just as our personal histories anchor us, so too does mindful budgeting anchor our present choices to a coherent narrative about who we are and where we want to go. This alignment is neither incidental nor easy; it demands continuous engagement and courage to confront uncomfortable truths about consumption habits. Yet this very process fosters *clarity*, a clear sense of purpose that transcends fleeting desires or external pressures. Through this lens, budgeting transcends spreadsheets to become a spiritual and emotional practice, weaving together practical stewardship and self-knowledge.

Importantly, this vision acknowledges the tension between living within capitalism and resisting its totalising tendencies. It refuses to idealise a world without money or market exchange but challenges the assumption that one must surrender autonomy to economic forces. This is a *conscious capitalism*—one in which individuals cultivate financial literacy and emotional intelligence as safeguards against exploitation and distraction. Rather than passive recipients of market logic, readers are invited to become active participants shaping their economic lives with intention and integrity.

The notion of *sovereignty* invoked here is both political and deeply personal. It gestures toward the reclamation of autonomy in contexts shaped by subscription economies designed for endless engagement and extraction. This reclamation requires new tools and rituals: periodic clarity checks, intentional unsubscribing, and reflective budgeting practices that foreground meaning over maximisation. By consciously sculpting budgets that serve identity and purpose, individuals can resist the erasure of selfhood often perpetuated by passive financial habits.

Moreover, reclaiming budgeting as an active practice reorients the relationship with time. Time poverty is a well-documented social phenomenon, disproportionately affecting those caught in cycles of financial precarity and overwork. Budgeting with an awareness of time's value invites readers to design lives that prioritise rest, creativity, and presence. This temporal dimension deepens budgeting's ethical stakes—it becomes not just about accumulation or restriction but about creating space for flourishing.

This approach also underscores the inseparability of financial clarity from emotional and psychological wellbeing. The act of remembering what matters disrupts anxiety, shame, and numbing that often accompany financial uncertainty or overwhelm. In this way, budgeting becomes a form of radical self-care—a practice that cultivates resilience and hope amid complexity.

Historical and cultural perspectives enrich this argument by revealing how societies have long grappled with the tension between economic necessity and personal autonomy. The contemporary subscription model, with its promise of convenience yet risk of entrapment, echoes earlier economic forms of servitude, yet offers new possibilities for liberation through conscious practice. Recognising these continuities and ruptures sharpens the critical gaze necessary for transformative budgeting.

Real-world examples further illuminate this vision. From individuals adopting 'subscription sabbaths' to communities organising financial literacy initiatives grounded in self-awareness, we see how budgeting can be revitalised as a practice of empowerment. These examples demonstrate that reclaiming budgeting is not theoretical but eminently practical, with tangible benefits for mental health, financial stability, and life satisfaction.

In navigating the future, readers are encouraged to cultivate *monthly clarity rituals*—intentional pauses that invite reflection, recalibration, and recommitment to values. These rituals serve as anchors, combating the dissociative effects of fast-paced consumption and supporting sustained engagement with one's budgetary story. Through disciplined remembering, budgeting becomes a dynamic conversation between past, present, and future selves.

Ultimately, this chapter articulates a profound truth: the future of budgeting hinges on our willingness to engage actively with the forces shaping our financial lives and to reclaim the narratives that ground us. It demands that we refuse passivity and instead embrace budgeting as a daily act of remembering who we are and what we stand for. Such clarity is not a destination but a continual practice—one that empowers readers to navigate complexity with intention, sovereignty, and hope.

About the Author

Evelyn Hawthorne is a behavioral finance specialist and mindful-living advocate with a deep-seated passion for revealing the invisible systems that shape our financial lives. Drawing on a decade of work blending cognitive psychology, consumer behavior research, and mindfulness practices, she brings a uniquely human perspective to the world of budgeting—one that moves beyond spreadsheets into the terrain of values, attention, and agency. Evelyn's previous writings for Mindful Pages Publishers have explored conscious money habits and the intersection of mental clarity and personal finance. In The Price of Forgetting, she leverages her insider understanding of subscription ecosystems and her skill in guiding readers toward compassionate self-awareness, offering not just strategies, but transformative insight.

www.ingramcontent.com/pod-product-compliance
Lightning Source LLC
Chambersburg PA
CBHW031350230926
51848CB00002B/467
* 9 7 8 9 3 7 1 7 7 1 5 1 1 *